Dollar Non¢ents

To Jan Brown
End the Fed!
Peter Allison
2/10

Dollar Non¢ents

The Respected Fraud and Beneficial Devastation of the Federal Reserve Corporation

Peter S. Allison

Aventine Press

First Edition

Published by Aventine Press
1023 4th Ave #204
San Diego CA, 92101
www.aventinepress.com

ISBN: 1-59330-207-X

Printed in the United States of America

To

my beloved wife, Alice,

for the joy and love

she has brought to my life.

Table of Contents

Foreword

This book grew out of a one-day faculty seminar prepared a number of years ago. Its slow metamorphosis into a book was driven by the realization that while there was an abundance of literature on the Federal Reserve, most of it was written from the perspective that "conspirators" have victimized the American people. But this view of the world is fundamentally foreign to Scripture. The historic reformed faith has long understood national disaster and economic servitude to be a sign of God's judgement. The proper response is confession and repentance. The goal of this study is to begin to apply Scripture to the monetary policy on which our economic life is based — specifically what, if any, was the sin that has led us to this sorry state of economic affairs and how do we begin the process of changing our economy to one that does not flagrantly transgress the eighth commandment prohibiting theft.

Invariably, whenever this material was presented, someone would ask, "So what do we do now?" For some time I did not have a Scriptural answer in which I was firmly and deeply convinced. I could talk all around the answer, I could sense the answer, and I knew what wasn't the answer; but when all the talking was done, I knew in my heart I had not provided a clear, actionable answer. Thus, this completed manuscript lay unpublished on my desk. I now offer a clear, actionable answer in the knowledge that much more needs to be said and the hope that others will do so.

By no stretch of the imagination is this an exhaustive coverage of money. But it is hoped that seeds will be planted in this generation that will begin to bear fruit in subsequent ones. In many ways, the 20th century represents a nadir of Christianity since the reformation of the 16th century. That century saw the church compromise on the authority and infallibility of scripture; tolerate unbelief of the Genesis account of creation; adopt feminism, teaching that women could work outside the home and hold civil and ecclesiastical positions of leadership and sending her daughters off to war; practice planned barrenness contrary to the cultural mandate of Genesis 1; and by and large become culturally irrelevant. The last generation has seen the church begin an unmistakable return to obedience in many of these areas. Should the Lord graciously sustain this new obedience, it is this writer's prayer that even this seemingly unmovable mountain of monetary fraud blighting our nation may also be cast down.

I would like to acknowledge the assistance of many people in reading this manuscript and offering helpful feedback. A very special thanks to Newlyn Allison and Nathan Oman for their generous donation of time and editorial expertise in reviewing this manuscript and to my children for their cheerful help in everything from scanning documents to fetching references.

Peter Allison
Houston, TX

Chapter 1

The Story of Stone Money

In the summer of 1903, a respected American anthropologist by the name of William Henry Furness III spent several months on an obscure speck of land in the South Pacific called the Island of Yap. The purpose of his visit was simply to learn more about the inhabitants of this little known island on the western edge of the Caroline Islands in Micronesia. Among all of the curious customs and fashions one would expect from a primitive culture, he was most intrigued by their system of money; so much so that he named his book about these people, *The Island of Stone Money*. There was no metal on the island and no technology to smelt ore even if it had been there. Instead, the Yaps used large rocks called *fei* as their money. These rocks, or *fei,* had been quarried on an island some 400 hundred miles away, shaped into large thick torroids or doughnuts, and then towed on rafts back to the Island of Yap several generations before.

What impressed Mr. Furness most about the Yap's system of money was the fact that the owner did not need to have physical possession of the *fei* in order for it to be considered his. For example, if a native received a *fei* in exchange for a boat, the new *fei* owner might very well leave the stone on the previous owner's property. For that matter, the stone he received may not have even been in the previous owner's possession. The physical location of the *fei* stone simply had no affect whatsoever on its purchasing power. According to Fatumak, the native that befriended Mr. Furness during his summer on the island, there was a family of great wealth in a neighboring village whose primary source of wealth was a *fei* of magnificent proportions. However, no one, not even the current owners, had ever set eyes on their wealth, for it had sunk in deep water several hundred miles from Yap in the course of being transported home. As the story goes, a storm had arisen and the navigators had been forced to cut the raft adrift in order to save their lives. Upon arriving home safely, the sailors unanimously testified to the exceptional quality of the stone and the to fact that it had been lost through no fault of its owners. Without further thought, it was universally conceded that a few hundred feet of water ought not to diminish its purchasing power in any way. Thus it remained as valuable on the ocean floor as if it had been sitting against the owner's house.[1]

This is not the end of the story. When the Germans bought the place in 1898, there were no roads on the island. Because the natives did not have any wheeled vehicles, they considered the existing paths that crossed the island entirely satisfactory for their bare feet and flatly ignored every government edict to upgrade the roads. The Germans were at a loss as to how they could compel the natives to rebuild the roads. The confiscation of money (a fine) would certainly not have any effect. After all, if the purchasing power of *fei* stones lost on the ocean floor was the same as if they were sitting on someone's front yard, their purchasing power would certainly not be impaired if they were carted off to Germany. Eventually, the German government discovered that the fine could be effected by placing a big black X on the *fei,* indicating that they were claimed by the German government. The people, believing they were thus impoverished, "turned to" and expeditiously rebuilt the roads, making them look like park drives. The German agents removed the X's, and the natives, now rolling in wealth, were once again happy. And they even had good roads.[2]

Figure 1. *Fei* stones on the Island of Yap

Before you laugh too hard at the naiveté of these poor peasants of Yap, ask yourself when you last saw your money. A critical analysis will reveal that our money system has only one real difference: we don't even bother with the stones. We prefer to use an intangible entity. We cannot even claim that our money is on the ocean floor.

President Garfield is reputed to have said that he who controls a nations volume of money was absolute master of their industry and commerce. He was not alone in this belief. In January, 1924, the chairman of the board of the Midland Bank, Reginald McKenna, told its stockholders, "I am afraid the ordinary citizen will not like to be told that the banks can, and do, create money ... And they who control the nations credit direct the policy of the Governments and hold in the hollow of their hands the destiny of the people."[3] If, according to President Garfield, there is an absolute master, then there also must be an absolute slave. This book is an attempt to explain who the absolute masters of the American economy are. I think you can guess who are the absolute slaves.

Before you dismiss the thought of masters and slaves in 21st century America as radical or extreme, consider the fact that the history of mankind is literally littered with men who have tried to conquer the world and enslave its inhabitants. One need only think of the ancient world empires of Egypt, Assyria, Babylon, Alexander the Great, or Rome or the more modern empires of Spain, England, France, or 20th Germany. Each of these empires was built by men intent on ruling the world. Each of them succeeded to varying degrees in conquering sizable sections of the known world. The threat of world-wide rule is not a recent invention of paranoid extremists. If anything, the surprise ought to be that we in America should have enjoyed several hundred years of relative freedom from such men and their plots for power. That freedom was the fruit of cultural obedience to the Word of God over successive generations, an obedience that was rooted in the reformation of the 16th century. But the sun is fast fading on that day of liberty. Like the natives of Yap who were enslaved by a black mark on their stones, you and I also exchange the fruit of our labor for an illusion.

Now I realize that you're probably thinking anything from a skeptical "What do you mean?" to outright derision. So let me be quick to add, yes, there is one difference between us and the natives of Yap who may never have seen their money: We don't even know *what* our money is! There is no tangible substance that anyone has been able to identify that is used as money today. If you could identify the substance that we use as money today, I would gladly give you one pound of it — absolutely free!

While helpful financial advisors might be asking, "Where is your money?", the more relevant question is, "*What* is your money?" Only after we know *what* we are looking for will we be able to determine where our money is.

Chapter 2

Money: Can You Feel It ?

Perhaps you have never found banking and money a very interesting or comprehensible aspect of your economics education, if you have even bothered with them at all. If so, don't skip this chapter; there is a simple reason for that, as we shall see. And it is not necessarily your fault. For although banking is often perceived or presented as being beyond the understanding of mere mortals, as something too complex to be comprehended by anyone other than high-level financiers running complicated models, the truth is quite the opposite. If you can read, I am certain that by the end this chapter you will know more than some professional economists. That is not saying as much as it would seem. In a later chapter, we will see that by their own admission, economists do not even know what our money is today.[4]

What is Money?

Now that I have castigated economists, you are quite likely asking me, "What is money?" Very simply, it is the most vendible, or the most marketable, commodity; it is something that "many" people value. An industrial air compressor is very valuable to a mechanic, and a fork truck is very useful in a warehouse, but neither are very marketable to a wide group of people. Would you trade all your household appliances for a construction-grade air compressor? Although these things are very valuable, the market for them is also relatively narrow. They are not very vendible. Commodity means that whatever is used *is* "something"; it must be tangible. You have to be able to touch it, smell it, hear it, taste it, or see it. There is no such thing as "a money" in and of itself. Just like there is no such thing as a furniture. These are abstract terms. There are things that we use as furniture. We use tables, chairs, beds, etc. as furniture. In the same way, there are commodities that we use as money. Exactly what commodity winds up being used as money depends entirely on the situation or what we would call the economy. The most vendible commodity for Robinson Crusoe is not the same as the most vendible commodity for us. The most vendible commodity is determined by the free market, which means it is determined by people as they freely trade. No government can specify what it will be.[5] Nowhere in Scripture is it specified what we must use as money.

Another satisfactory definition, offered by A. Barton Hepburn, is, "Sound money means money made of (or unquestionably redeemable in) a commodity which has a stable value in the markets of the world independent of fiat. Sound money as applied to paper or token money of any kind means that which is redeemable in money wherein the commercial value of its bullion equals it coinage value."[6] Apart from using the word to be defined in the definition, this otherwise satisfactory definition also contains the key points that money is a commodity and if paper is used in place of this commodity, there must be a one-to-one correspondence between the paper and the commodity which it represents.

Choice of Commodity used as Money

Robinson Crusoe provides us with an example in which gold was definitely not the most vendible commodity. Gary North, in his book *Honest Money,* provides a very helpful analysis of this famous fictional economy of one. Initially, Crusoe faced a desperate situation. He was stranded on an island with nothing but what he salvaged off of a sinking ship. In doing this, he had to make some hard choices. His crude raft would only hold so many items. What should he take? In making those choices, Crusoe had to impute subjective value to each item, a value that had nothing to do with its original cost. Crusoe probably passed by an expensive sextant or oil painting hanging in the captain's cabin in favor of cheaper items like seeds for planting, a knife, a shovel, or any number of other tools that would help him make what he needed. The sextant and the painting were worthless to him. The simple tools were much more valuable, despite the fact that, originally, the sextant cost far more than the knife. The cost of production or the original selling price had nothing to do with an object's value. Rather value was based entirely on Crusoe's subjective estimation of an item's expected future output or utility.[7]

The objective conditions around Crusoe, such as the conditions on the island, the strength of his raft, or the weather at the time all figured into his evaluation. But he alone determined value and allocated the scarce resources accordingly—either leaving them on the sinking ship or putting them on his raft. In this scenario, gold had absolutely no value. It is worthless in this situation: "gold is heavy, it displaces tools, and sinks [small] rafts. It is not only useless to Crusoe, it is a liability."[8] Value is based on expectation of future output. All that gold can do for a man alone on the island is to remain alone on the island with him. In a different set of circumstances, the same person might impute an entirely different value to the same objects. Value literally can and does change with the weather.

We can also look at a non-fictional example in which gold was not the most vendible commodity. During Joseph's day, there was a great famine in Egypt. Conditions were so bad the Scriptures (Genesis 47) tell us that the money failed.[9] How does money fail? If you were a farmer in those days eating your last bag of wheat, would you sell it for a bag of gold? Of course not. You cannot eat gold coins, and they are not very fun to count when your arms have become so emaciated that you lack the strength to lift them. Relative to grain, the money or gold and silver was worth next to nothing. Gold ceased to be the most vendible commodity. Grain, being more vendible than gold, was now being used as money. Everyone would have been interested in grain. If they themselves did not need it, then they would have been confident that they could find someone who did.

Many other things have been used as money in the world. Roman soldiers were paid with salt, which is where our word salary comes from. If a soldier was not worth his wages, then he was said not to be worth his salt, an expression that continues today. Seashells, fishhooks, opium, cows, and, in the not too distant past in the not too distant state of colonial Virginia, tobacco have all been used as money. That does not mean that people walked around with tobacco leaves neatly folded in their wallets with various numbers inscribed thereon. They would have stored their tobacco in warehouses and traded the deposit receipts for it—at least for a few transactions. Eventually, someone would go to the warehouse with the receipt, take out the tobacco, and either use it or trade it to someone who would use it.

But all of these commodities have severe shortcomings and have long ceased to be used as money by commercial nations. Tobacco can only be stored so long before it is useless for smoking. If cows are being used as money, there is a problem with divisibility. It is hard to make change with a cow. If your neighbor comes to you with four pigs wanting to trade them for your cow, Bossy, then you might be able to make a deal, assuming you were willing to trade a cow for four pigs. But what if you only wanted two pigs? "Not a problem," your neighbor assures you as he approaches your Bossy with his gigantic meat saw, "I can make change." There is a problem: two halves are definitely less than a whole.

For the most part, these are the exceptional cases. Under most circumstances, in most societies for the last several millennia, gold and silver have emerged as the most vendible commodities. Gold vendors have never needed to stand in the streets, begging people to buy their gold. Instead they have usually had to hire armed guards to keep people from stealing it. "Men chose gold and silver for the material for money, for reasons similar to those which induced them to choose wool, flax, silk, and cotton for materials for clothing, and stone brick, and timber for materials for building. Gold and silver had those specific qualities which fitted them to be standards and measures of value..."[10] They are easily divisible, relatively portable, very durable, and have a uniformity of quality all over the world. In fact there is only one acid, aqua regia, that can destroy gold. Gold is also easily recognized. You can determine its purity with only a beaker of water and a scale. Furthermore, it is scarce. You cannot simply go out and dig hunks out of the ground or pick it off trees. While gold and silver are not the only commodities that could be used as money, they are the most convenient.

Value and Utility of Money in an Economy

Money is a vital part of society because it greatly enhances trade, which is what makes the division of labor possible. Division of labor is what makes the middle class in America possible today. Without it, you simply have the rich and the poor: those who have slaves to do their work and those who must do it themselves. If we had to produce everything that we use ourselves, most of us would just be finishing breakfast by the time the sun set. But when there is trade, you and I no longer have to make everything we use. Where trade is easy, people can become very good in one area—maybe it is in physics, maybe lawn mowing, maybe repairing cars—and then trade the product of their skill for this "most vendible commodity" that we call money. Everyone knows that because it is so very marketable, they will be able to take this money to anyone, anywhere, and trade it for something else that they need. Having money makes that in-between trade far less risky and, hence, something that people will do far more readily.

For example, assume that I, a specialist at making computers, want to obtain a suit, and that you, a physicist, want a computer. I can build a computer and exchange it with you for the commodity being used as money. I can then go to the tailor, who can make suits more quickly than most other people, and trade this commodity that we are using as money for a suit. The amazing thing about a free market is that you get your computer with less work than if you yourself had made it, and I get my suit with less work then if I made it myself. The same is true of the tailor. Consequently, everybody gains. Production is higher overall, even though nobody is working any longer hours. Higher production with less time invested results in a higher standard of living for everyone.

If there was no money, then I would only be able to trade with people that had suits and needed a computer. Or, in order to get my suit, I would need to visit the tailor and find out what he wanted. Maybe he wants a violin. Then I would have to locate a person that would be willing to trade a violin for a computer, so that I could then go to the tailor to trade the violin for the suit. As you can see, this gets very complicated. It becomes easier just to make the suit myself, or find someone in my family to make it. Without money, trade is difficult. Without money, I cannot even begin to trade with you, the physicist, because the market for your skills is extremely limited. But with a universally vendible commodity, or money, all of these trade problems are solved. Division of labor becomes practical, and everyone benefits; our economy as a whole benefits, and everyone's standard of living increases over what it would have been had we been forced to do everything ourselves. It is productivity (the cost to produce an item) that raises the standard of living in a society. It is not the number of new jobs, nor the amount of income you get each month, nor the amount of money in circulation; nor is it the unemployment rate that determines the health and wealth of a nation. It is increased productivity.

Money is the most vendible commodity. It is a tangible object: *something* that is extended in space. Having a commodity that is universally accepted greatly simplifies trade, thereby increasing productivity (less effort to make a trade), which in turn increases real wealth. Because money facilitates the division of labor, money makes possible increased productivity. It gives people options. It gives people greater freedom. It allows people to compare the value of pigs and violins, because their value can now be expressed in terms of the same commodity. One tenth of an ounce of gold for a pig, a full ounce for a violin. This ease in economic comparison streamlines trade and reduces the risks inherent in trading. This increases production while reducing the losses from bad trades. Money also allows people to save up their productivity in a commodity that is both marketable and durable. If you were a vegetable farmer, it would be very difficult to save your work for a rainy day. But if you can convert your vegetables into a durable commodity like gold, you can stockpile your labor. When your children come to clean out the mattress they will find more than a pile of rotten vegetables or some other commodity that has lost its market value — such as pile of vacuum tubes or buggy wheels.

Chapter 3

Fraudulent Money and Banking: The Bane of All Liberty

If mankind were not sinful, we could stop our study of economics right here and live happily ever after. But because of the Fall, things have become far more interesting. Men have an irrepressible love of the glitter of gold, and the history of the world is the history of men seeking more gold and more wealth. Greedy kings wage wars to acquire money, and greedy peasants clip coins. That is why coins have ridges on them. They make it obvious when a coin has been clipped or shaved, because the ridges will be missing or not as pronounced. You, the merchant, don't have to accept a coin that has been clipped. God, knowing the wicked heart of man, declared in Leviticus 19:35–36 that we should do no injustice in judgment, in measurements of length, weight, or volume. God commands us to have just balances (scales), just weights, a just ephah, and a just hin. Rest assured that the proverbial "thumb on the scale" is not a problem limited to dishonest butchers. It plagues bankers as well. The only difference is that bankers have acquired great cunning in disguising their thumb, so that it does not look like a thumb when it rests on the scale. Henry Hazlitt, a economic journalist for the *Wall Street Journal* once said, "Economics is haunted by more fallacies than any other study known to man."[11] He was not exaggerating. He is even more correct today. This chapter will be spent discerning these fallacies so that we can recognize the thumb sitting upon our monetary scale.

The Thumb on the Scale Problem

Suppose you had acquired a nest egg of gold coins from a life of diligent labor. What would you do with them? Where would you save them? This is no trivial question. Mattresses are fairly common places to hide gold coins; but you might not feel too safe putting it there. Better options would be to bury it in your back yard, hire a mason to build you a big vault, or you could pay your friend Honest Bruno to safe keep it for you. He is bonded and already has a large vault, security guards, TV cameras—the works. You trust him to give it back to you when you want it; after all, he is a reputable businessman. Of course, you still require him to give you a contract to cover the transaction: you give him 100 ounces of gold coin, and he gives you a receipt stating that you have 100 ounces of gold coin on deposit in his warehouse. Or he might give you 10 identical receipts that read, "Honest Bruno will pay to the bearer on demand 10 ounces in gold coin." Now you can sleep much better knowing that your life's labor is safe from thieves or at least most thieves. Occasionally, you might check on it or even remove some or add to it. But for the most part, it just sits there waiting for the day your heirs claim it or the day you need a bigger house. Other people do the same thing. They take their gold to a warehouse for safekeeping and receive a receipt for it in exchange. One day, you decide that the time has arrived to build the bigger barn. You settle on a price with your builder, but the warehouse is not open that day. So you inform your builder, "I'll pay you on Monday when Honest Bruno's warehouse opens."

The builder replies, "Well, actually, I bank with Honest Bruno too. Why don't you just give me your receipts? That will save you a trip, and I can take the receipts to Honest Bruno and get the gold myself as I need it."

Sounds like a good deal, and it is.

Rigging the Scales of Trade

As the practice of trading receipts for gold in place of the actual gold became commonplace, historically, bankers found that rarely, if ever, did anyone come to get the gold coins. They mostly sat in the corner collecting dust. What do you suppose Honest Bruno does with this pile of gold? What do you suppose a sinner will do with a pile of gold sitting in his house that nobody ever comes to claim? Why not loan it out — at interest, no less. Bankers found that they too could loan out the gold that was deposited with them and make interest on it, in addition to the fee that they were collecting for its storage.[12] Sounds like a smart move, getting double use out of the money. Aside from the fact that Honest Bruno has broken his contract with you and loaned out your money that he had promised to store, we now we have another problem. The same money is being used in two different places at the same time. Wouldn't you also like to get double the use out of your car and be able to go two places at once in it? By loaning the gold while the receipts were circulating, Honest Bruno has just doubled the available money in the marketplace. You are trading the receipt for the gold and someone else is out trading the actual gold. That is a deception and a fraud. It is as deceptive as making coins that claim to be one ounce of gold but are really half an ounce of gold and half an ounce of copper. As with any fraud, there are bad consequences. God is not mocked. Money is a commodity, something that is extended in space. It cannot be in two places at once any more than your car can be in two places at once.

We live in a world of scarcity. Honest Bruno cannot double the amount of money in circulation without expending any time or money. We do not get things for free. Not even our salvation was free. Someone had to pay the price. Someone will pay the price for this fraud as well. To see who pays, let us go back to Robinson Crusoe's island and imagine that it now contains a city with a stable economy. They trade exclusively with themselves using red rocks as money. These descendants of Robinson Crusoe have habitually traded one red rock for a gallon of milk and around 5000 red rocks for an average home. Suppose one of Robinson's offspring goes to bed contemplating whether to purchase a new computer or a new suit. He has only enough money for one item, not both. Suppose further that one night while he is in dreamland, we were to fly a helicopter over the island and drop red rocks into everyone's yard, so as to exactly double their money. Would we double the wealth of the island? Even a casual observer will quickly realize that we have not doubled their wealth at all. Wealth is only increased when productivity is increased. We have not increased their productivity, we have not enabled them to manufacture widgets more quickly, or to raise more food on less land with less manpower. When they wake up the next morning, they will simply find that they have twice the number of rocks on hand than they had before. For many centuries in most countries, people have on average maintained about 5 weeks of cash on hand. [Real income is always measured by the amount of time it takes to earn it.] If we assume that these people do the same, then our helicopter expedition will have doubled their cash reserves to 10 weeks. If they simply held onto the extra money, nothing would happen. But is that what you would do if someone suddenly doubled the amount of money you had? Probably not. You would run out and try to spend it.[13] If you had no needs at the present time, the extra money would soon create a new need. If Robinson's descendants had previously maintained 5 weeks of cash reserves, that was because they did not consider the benefit of having $1.00 in additional cash reserves to be worth the sacrifice of spending one dollar less. There is no reason this perception will change. The islanders will try to spend the extra money. They will try to reduce their cash balances to their former level by spending more than they receive. When our friend wakes up the next morning and discovers his good fortune, he will initially think that he can now buy both the suit and the computer instead of having to choose between the two. Indeed, if he is one of the first few buyers in the marketplace the next day, he will get a steal; he can buy both the computer and the suit. What he might not realize is that everyone else also has twice as much money. Throughout the island, people are buying twice as much; twice as many suits are being sold, twice as many computers are being sold, twice as many of everything is being sold. Business is booming.

So far, this does not sound like a problem at all. It actually sounds rather good — too good to be true. As more than one wise person has said, "If it sounds to good to be true, it probably is." What they are not remembering is that one person's expenditure is another person's receipt. The members of the community as a whole cannot spend more than the community as a whole receives. Individuals as a whole cannot spend a balance; they can only circulate the money. They can only transfer a balance, not spend it. One person can spend more than he receives only if someone else is receiving more than he is spending. Thus, their attempts to spend this larger balance will be frustrated. But they will continue to try to spend a balance. What will happen in the process? Remember, nobody doubled the number of computers and suits sitting in the warehouses, and nobody doubled the rate at which suits and computers can be produced. Because everything is selling at twice the previous stable rate, inventories are soon depleted, and very quickly, there are no more suits or computers available — or anything else for that matter. Remember dropping rocks never increased anyone's productivity. The tailor can't make suits any faster and the computer manufacturer can't assemble computers any faster than they did before. Since the production of computers had previously matched the demand for computers, now it won't be able to keep up. In fact, no manufacturer will be able to keep up; and no service provider will be able to keep up with the new demands for his services, demands fueled by the additional money floating around.

Why is demand up? Because the heart of man is never satisfied with possessions, Scripture tells us. We always want more. Merchants are out of stock because the goods are bought as soon as they reach the shelf; providers of services are backlogged. After six trips to the computer store to purchase a computer, only to find someone had gotten there ahead of them; people will start offering the computer manufacturer a premium in order to get the next computer that's made. People will start offering to pay the carpet cleaner more to clean their carpets this week instead of next month. Remember, everyone has plenty of money. It is no problem to pay more. In a free market, where there are no controls on what people can do, the prices will rise to make the demand equal to the supply. If you don't believe this, go to any socialized country where price controls are holding the price down and see if there are not shortages. See for yourself if the government does not have to outlaw paying more for goods and services than the allowed price. Then, go into the back alleys and see if there is not a black market where the same goods are available and trading at much higher prices. Or just look at the number of Canadians who come to America and pay our "outrageous" medical prices to get medical service this month, instead of two years from now.

People will be forced to do without or pay a premium because nothing has happened yet to increase the available goods and services. As the price goes up, people will have to begin choosing between the suit and the computer. They will not have money for both. Some will choose a suit, and others will choose a computer; but the demand for both will fall until it matches the available supply. In a *laissez faire* market, where there are no controls restricting the freedom of people to act in the marketplace as they see fit (i.e., where people are not restricted in their freedom to choose), this process will occur rapidly. Prices will rise, which will decrease demand until the demand is once again equal to the supply. When all is said and done, the effect of our doubling the number of red rocks on our imagined island will be nothing more than to cut the value of each red rock in half. The effect of this is that while it once took 100 rocks to obtain 1 suit, it will now take 200 rocks to get the same suit. You recognize this as inflation. The cause of inflation is the devaluation of the money. The effect of this devaluation of money is that it now takes more worthless money to obtain the same commodities as before. There really is no free lunch.

**someone got nothing for something
so that someone else could get something for nothing**

If we go back to Honest Bruno, the clever banker who doubled the money supply with his loan of stored gold, we can see that the effect of his fraud will be a subsequent increase in prices. Eventually, wages, which are the price of labor, will go up as well. Some people might be tempted to think that other than the inconvenience of rising prices, no one really loses; so what is the great harm? They think that if their salary goes up at the same rate of inflation, they are not losing anything. Are they? *If* prices uniformly and instantly doubled everywhere at once, then there might some truth to this argument. However, nothing in the real world ever works instantly. It takes a finite time for information to move. Even light takes a finite time to travel from one point to another. A simple analysis will show that someone got something for nothing so that someone else could get nothing for something. Our friend was able to buy both a suit and a computer. The tailor and the computer dealer were paid with devalued red rocks.[14] Someone labored for produce that they did not receive so that someone else could receive produce for which they did not labor. That is theft. It is theft that particularly victimizes the widows, the poor, and the fatherless. (Scripture reserves particularly severe judgments for those who oppress these people.) Some Biblical sense ought to start whispering in your ear that no one can perpetrate a fraud like this and be guiltless. Remember, sin brings judgment. But where is it in this scenario?

Effects of Inflation

There are several problems in our scenario. The most obvious is the turmoil that is created in the marketplace by the infusion of money. It sends false signals about the actual demand for goods and services. While prices are reaching their new equilibrium level, manufacturers and service providers begin working overtime to increase production in an effort to keep up. With demand falling and production increasing, a surplus will develop before the price finally settles at its new level. The money tied up in surplus inventory represents money that is idle and not generating income for its owner. If there is a continual infusion of devalued money, then these false signals are much stronger and persistent and continually propagate throughout the economy. Additional employees may be hired to meet increased demand only to be laid off a little later, when there is an inevitable downturn in their industry. Families get thrown around as Father gets hired and then laid off. Everybody suffers, complaining of the tough business conditions which are simply the result of these conflicting market signals. If the downswings in the economy are big enough, it will be labeled a recession or panic. As will be shown in a later chapter, the amount of counterfeit money in circulation in the American economy is highly influenced by the interest rate. By manipulating the interest rate, and thus, the amount of counterfeit money, the American economy can be plunged into a recession at the pleasure of those controlling the interest rates.

Cash Balances Reduced And Replaced By Productive Resources[15]

If we complicate our scenario and make this dropping of red rocks a continually occurring process, then we add another problem. There is now a fee associated with the storage of money that arises when the money supply is being continually devalued. If my money, at the end of the year, is only worth 90% of what it was at the beginning of the year; I have paid a cost of 10% of my total cash reserves simply to hold the money one year. But by lowering my cash reserves I can now lower my storage expense and have more money available for spending. Every dollar that is spent is a dollar on which I do not have to pay the 10% storage fee. Under these circumstances, it only makes sense to attempt to spend more and hold less in reserve. Except remember that not everyone can spend more and reduce their reserves. So all that happens is that prices are bid up still further and people are left with lower real reserves. By real reserves, we mean lower purchasing power. Numbers may be higher, but the money will buy less. Thus, inflation reduces savings. This reduction in savings produces a subtle effect in itself. Real cash reserves or savings are themselves a part of production. Savings are the source of capital for new business ventures. Now, there is less real capital available, which means people have to borrow more to be able to embark on capital intensive programs, such as building. Although this is fine for the people on the loaning side, it is an additional cost for the borrowing business. The well-known result is that the rich get richer and the poor get poorer.

This cost of storage shows its ugly head in many other ways as well. A retailer will now tend to hold less cash on hand for making change. After all, it costs him to hold cash. He may find that it is cost effective to hire a courier to get change from the bank. When it costs 10 cents instead of nothing to hold a dollar for a year, it is cost effective to hire the courier. Now we have productive capability that is not going into production. The courier does not help the retailer sell any more merchandise in a year. His labor has not resulted in increased production and, thus, does not help to raise the overall wealth of a nation. His service is a consumptive service that is accepted as a cost of doing business.[16] Inflation has caused cash balances to be replaced by non-productive resources, in this case a courier service. God will not be mocked. You cannot perpetrate a fraud and expect to escape without penalty. The consequence of the principle of scarcity will exact its due on society. God's holy commands concerning just weights and measures have been violated, and the consequences must be borne by you and me. The next time you are tempted to complain about rising prices or having to work harder to earn the same purchasing power, remember that we are only reaping what our parents have sown.

Unequal Distribution Effects

But there is yet another problem with increasing the supply of paper money without increasing productivity or labor. In a more realistic scenario, unlike our helicopter example, the money is not instantly distributed equally to everyone. It is introduced into the market at one point. This means that the person who gets the money first gets an unjust advantage over everyone else. He gets to play in the marketplace at today's prices with tomorrow's money. In effect, he is really stealing from the first merchants he patronizes. They are giving up their products in exchange for paper receipts that are not worth what they used to be worth. What our Honest Bruno has done is no different than a counterfeiter printing up receipts in his basement and spending them in the marketplace. When the counterfeiter obtains the products of merchants with his counterfeited receipts, he is obtaining goods without paying for them. He gets something for nothing. If he is getting something for nothing, someone else is getting nothing for something. Remember there is no free lunch. Somebody had to produce everything that is for sale in the marketplace. They are entitled to just compensation for their labor. But they do not receive just compensation when people can obtain it with counterfeited or devalued money. Unlike the first people to receive the devalued money, the last people to get the money have to pay today's prices with yesterday's money. Who are these people? They are the ones farthest from the bank. Often they are the poor who cannot get loans from the bank. By dumping duplicate receipts into the marketplace, wealth can be transferred from the last people to receive the devalued money to the people that obtained the devalued money first. That is theft just as surely as counterfeiting with a printing press.

Duplicate Paper Receipts — The Greatest Deception Since the Forbidden Fruit

But this is just the beginning of our troubles. Honest Bruno, our clever but maybe not so honest banker friend, soon discovers another trick.

Bankers found that they did not actually have to loan the gold sitting in their stockpile if they could convince borrowers to accept merely the receipt for the gold. Figure 2 shows an example of this type of bank note. You bring Banker Bruno your 100 ounces of gold, and he gives you a receipt in exchange, which you proceed to use in trade. Now a borrower comes along later on that afternoon and wants to borrow the gold. Instead of receiving the gold, he simply receives a receipt just like you received. After all, if the receipt is good enough for you, the owner of the gold, why should it not be good enough for him? You do not have to be a genius to see where this is leading. There is now no limit on the number of loans that Bruno can make. He can make money flow like water. His generosity can produce the biggest economic boom that anyone has ever seen. All the while, he can collect interest many times

Figure 2. Receipt For 10 Dollars of Coined Gold Deposited With The US Treasury.[17]

over on the same pile of gold. Pretty slick. Don't you think Avis would like to be able to collect rent from 10 different people on the same car at the same time and never have the car leave the garage? Most people would probably consider that fraud and expect the government to lock them in jail. But when bankers successfully do the same thing with gold (which they do not even own), the same people consider them successful businessmen and vote them into esteemed civil offices of influence and leadership.[18]

Fractional Reserve Banking — Another Name For Duplicate Paper Receipts

This, by the way, is called fractional reserve banking—putting more receipts for gold into circulation than there is actual gold. Banks have been doing it for centuries, but no banker has yet gone to jail for it in this country, to the best knowledge of this author. That does not make it right anymore than our government's legalization of abortion makes abortion lawful. Bruno could go on giving out receipts for your gold, and no one would be the wiser—until someone returns to claim his gold. Now Banker Bruno has a problem. There are countless receipts floating around out there, each of which contains his promise to give the pile of gold to the bearer. All it takes is for two of them to come back claiming their gold for the secret to be out that there is no more gold in Honest Bruno's vault. Herein lies the challenge for all who would engage in fractional reserve banking: maintaining a universal faith in the intrinsic value of their paper IOUs.

What would you do if you heard via news report that all of the jewelry had been stolen from the local jeweler where you had just dropped off your diamond solitaire for repair? Would you not pay the jeweler a visit to see if your ring was still there? When everyone runs to the bank demanding their gold, it is called a run on the bank. But, of course, there is not enough gold at the bank for everyone; so Bruno has to close his doors and declare bankruptcy. In some cultures, he may also have been executed. Historically, bank runs happen with alarming regularity where fractional reserve banking is practiced; and, despite the Federal Reserve Bank's best efforts, it still happens today. There was a run on a major bank in Maryland in late 1985. The lobbies were jammed with people trying to get their money. Eventually, it closed its doors and many people were unable to access their funds for months.

When a bank is unable to redeem their deposit receipts, everybody left holding the worthless receipts loses, unless they have a wood stove and can use the paper to heat their houses. They may have performed work and received one of Bruno's receipts. Or they may have parted with merchandise in exchange for one of Bruno's worthless receipts. Now, all they are holding is a piece of paper that no one will take. They are victims of theft. They have received nothing for their labor so that someone else could get something for nothing. We might ask a question for reflection. Is there any real difference after the bank run than there was before? This writer would say, "Not really." If people are defrauded, then they were defrauded before as well. The only difference was their level of trust in the bank.

The Government Gets in on the Action

It is bad enough when private banks counterfeit their own currency. But at least it is a level playing field. Other people can counterfeit as well, and those who choose not to participate in the fraud can do that just as easily. When the fraudulent bank fails, a few foolish depositors will be hurt, but the economy as a whole will be untouched. Even the people who lose their money have a good prospect of recovering quickly. But what is far worse is when a government wants to get a piece of the action. The government has several weapons in its arsenal that makes its counterfeiting much more disastrous and deadly to the nation than the penny ante stuff a local bank can do. The government has the power of the sword behind it. They can force everyone to accept their worthless receipts, which we call *fiat* money — something that would not happen in a free market. Literally, *fiat* money is money by decree. It is much more difficult to refrain from participating in the fraud or to be immune to the consequences when Uncle Sam legalizes counterfeiting.

When the government goes to bed with the bankers, nobody's freedom is safe. Government uses the power of the sword to protect the monopoly of banks to counterfeit money by fractional reserve banking. In return, bankers are not prosecuted for fraud when they issue promises to pay while never intending to pay. Bankers are protected by government police from citizens that come demanding their money. Why do governments do this? They protect the bankers because fractional reserve banking provides them access to free money: money that they do not have to directly tax from the people. It makes for a tight marriage.

Over the centuries, many governments, including our own at various times and places, have done this. In Marco Polo's day, governments did not bother with the banks. They just printed the money themselves. Marco Polo wrote about how the reigning Chinese ruler stole his citizen's time and labor by counterfeiting.[19] In the same way, our government, through fraudulent banks, has used *fiat* money to confiscate our wealth in order to finance its dreams. Houses that are not built in obedience to word of God are houses built on sand. We know what Jesus said about the houses built on sand: they will fall and great will be their fall. The same is true of banks built on fraud. When they fall, fraudulent central banks bring nations to their knees with them.

Even though the government would prosecute Avis for fraud if they rented the same car to 10 people at the same time, they do let banks rent out their gold to 10 people at the same time. Why? Because you can't punish someone caught with their hand in the till when your hand is in there at the same time. Not even the Pharisees dared to do that.

John Maynard Keynes, the perverted homosexual and author of an equally perverted economic theory, understood this quite clearly. In 1920, he wrote in *Economic Consequences of the Peace*,

> By a continuous process of inflation governments can confiscate, secretly and unobserved, an important part of the wealth of their citizens. By this method, they not only confiscate, but they confiscate *arbitrarily*; and while the process impoverishes many, it actually enriches some... There is no subtler, no surer means of overturning the existing basis of society than to debauch the currency. The process engages all the hidden forces of economic law on the side of destruction, and does so in a manner in which not one man in a million can diagnose.[20]

Just look at the intense dislike and distrust of the government that exists today in early 21st century America. It is a sign of the overturning of the existing basis of society to which Keynes referred. He also called inflation an easy tax to enforce, one that a weak government can enforce when they can enforce no other; a tax that can be levied even when the people would never permit Congress to pass a tax hike. For example: everybody holds money. You may not hold the same piece of paper, but over the course of a year, everyone holds a significant amount of money. If someone earns $48,000 in a year, not only are they holding $4,000 for the better part of each month, but they also probably have several thousand dollars in savings. If inflation is 10% annually, they are being taxed $400 each year just by virtue of the money that passes through their hands. Of course, if more money is held, the tax is proportionally greater. The fact that one is earning 10% interest does not reduce this tax. But the biggest tax is in the money that they have not yet received. The price of their labor was established at the start of the year. The employee in our example will receive $48,000 for a year of labor. By the end of the year, that price is effectively 10% less. In the above example, this amounts to a tax of some $2400. A tax that never shows up on anyone's balance sheet. A tax, according to Keynes, that not one man in a million is even aware of paying. But a tax whose consequences, nevertheless, are very real. It is a tax on the productivity of people before that labor is even converted into money, resulting in people having to expend more and more labor to achieve the same financial reward.

In extreme cases, it is even a tax on people after their labor is converted into money. In 1925, Mr. Attilio Eneiui of Portland, Oregon, received a letter from a German bank where he had one million marks on deposit. The bank told him:

> By reason of the new bank act and the new mint law of August 30th, 1924 the new Reichsmark currency has been established in Germany on October 11th, 1924. The Reichsmark is now legal tender in the country. In accordance with the Mint Law one Reichsmark of the new currency is equal to one billion (1,000,000,000,000) marks of the former currency.[21]
>
> With the establishment of the new Reichsmark as legal tender, we had to introduce the Reichsmark in our bookkeeping system. On December 31st 1923 your account showed a balance of Papermarks 1,000,000 in your favor, and as this amount cannot be expressed in the smallest units of the new currency, a conversion into Reichsmark is impossible. The balance on your account has in fact been wiped out by the depreciation of the mark and by part of the charges for carrying the account since

the last statement we sent to you. For these reasons we must to our great regret, inform you that we were obliged to close your old Mark account on our books.[22]

One million marks would have bought a nice house just after World War I. After inflation, it was not even enough to keep a bank account open. That man lost a house to the tax of inflation. This type of inflation was present more recently in several Latin American and South-American countries. During January of 1995, Mexico's peso lost 30% of its value in just a couple of weeks. The *Wall Street Journal* told about a lady from Brazil who, after suffering through a half dozen failed currencies, was finally able to take her children to Disneyland because Brazil had a paper money that was not hyper-inflating for the first time in her life.[23]

People feel the effect of this tax, even if they may not be able to diagnose its cause, and they act accordingly. If it costs money to hold money, then any intelligent person will hold less money. This is exactly what many Americans are doing. Between 1980 and 2000 the personal savings rate declined from around 10% to 1%.

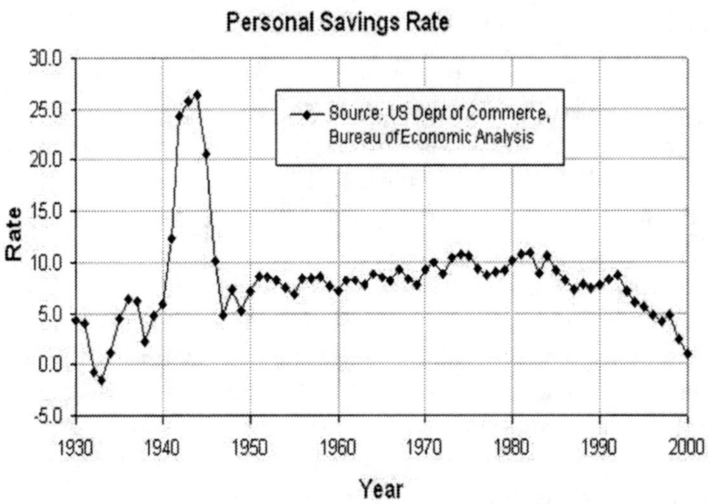

Figure 3. Personal Savings Rate

Maybe you are wondering who is receiving this tax? That is a good question over which some people have scratched their heads and others have confidently answered. Because private corporations are involved, it is hard to name specific individuals, although we will attempt it in a later chapter. The generic answer is the people who are able to receive and spend the *fiat* money first — usually the government. This tax, as I have illustrated it, does not sound too high. If you go by the published inflation rate, that is true. However, I would submit that the actual rate of inflation is much greater. The published rate of inflation does not take into account the brilliant inventions of the last 100 years (e.g., plastics, radios), or the cost-saving measures manufacturers have implemented. Plumbing pipes are made of plastic instead of galvanized steel. Cars, filing cabinets, and lawnmowers are made of thinner metal and have plastic parts in places that formerly had metal ones. One cannot simply compare the cost of a filing cabinet today with the cost 20 years ago. One also has to take into account the amount of steel and labor used in each cabinet. Robots and automated manufacturing equipment have actually greatly reduced the cost of production. Prices should be falling sharply. The fact that they are rising at even 1–2% per year signifies a high real inflation rate. When this is taken into account, the actual inflation rate will be seen to be many, many times greater than the published rate.

One could also look at the production of food. A generation or so ago, a nice sized family farm was 160 acres. Today, no family could live on the produce of only 160 acres. Is that because the 160-acre farm no longer produces as much as it used to? No. If anything, it actually produces far more today because farmers are generally more efficient than they used to be. Then why can't a family live on 160 acres? It is because a bag of potatoes is far cheaper today than it used to be. Formerly, a bag of potatoes might have been worth one hour of the farmer's time. Today that same bag might be worth only one minute of a farmer's time due to the great improvements in productivity. In real, uninflated dollars, the price of food has actually fallen drastically in the last 50 years. Yet, when you go to the local grocery store, you find the price of food has gone up. Why? The answer is that the actual inflation rate is far greater than the price increase you have seen at the grocery store. It is this actual inflation rate at which you are being taxed. It is this tax of which Keynes says that not one man in a million is able to comprehend.

Inflation is theft. Inflation is a tax. It is a tax authorized by no known law and for which no elected body will claim responsibility. This leads to the simple conclusion that inflation constitutes taxation without representation. What would Patrick Henry or Thomas Jefferson say about that?

We are not left to our imagination in answering this question. In the late 18th century, the colonies experienced some of the worst hyperinflation any nation has known. Fortunately, they learned from their mistakes, and America profited from that wisdom for over 100 years. But there is another reason for considering the perspective of this country's Founding Fathers: it brings an outside perspective to our discussion today. Is this chapter simply another "Chicken Little" crying that the sky is falling? Or, are duplicate paper receipts really as wrong as this chapter is suggesting?

Chapter 4

Banking and the Founding Fathers

The colonists brought very little gold and silver with them when they first came to this country. Since there were no gold or silver mines, there was very little precious metal used as money, and very little demand for it. Instead, they traded a wide variety of commodities, such as tobacco, rice, and furs. Each colony experimented with various laws to standardize the relative values of these commodities, but with minimal success. Only one colony, Massachusetts, established a mint with the intent of using gold and silver coin as money. But that ran afoul of the Motherland. "Vigorous attempts were made to force the managers to pay a portion of the profits to the government, but with little success, and in 1684 the mint was closed by order of the Crown."[24] Shortly afterwards, the colonies began experimenting with paper notes.

However, they were not very sophisticated about it. They simply got out their printing presses and started cranking out pieces of paper with pretty pictures on them. In 1736, we find Benjamin Franklin apologizing for getting his Pennsylvania Gazette out late. His explanation: "the printer was 'with the Press, labouring for the publick Good, to make Money more plentiful.'"[25] He called it a labor for the public good because printing paper money was thought to be a desirable alternative to taxes; a painless way to pay soldiers or meet any other financial obligation. One member of congress is even quoted by Pelatiah Webster as saying, "Do you think, gentlemen, that I will consent to load my constituents with taxes, when we can send to the printer, and get a whole wagonload of money."[26] As a more astute observer might expect, uncontrolled printing of paper receipts by each state and competing bank resulted in an financial train wreck.

Even the Founding Fathers, generally renowned for their civil wisdom, in desperate straits to finance the war, resorted to the tax that any government, no matter how weak, can enforce, and they printed IOU's or promises to pay gold and silver. The only problem was that they had very little silver and gold with which to make good on their promises to pay. Oh, they still paid very dearly for their ignorance, but not in gold and silver. By 1779, the Continental Congress had issued over 240 million dollars of IOU notes. This had the same effect as the hypothetical red rocks dumped our imaginary island. People bid up the price of goods and services until it took 225 of the paper notes to buy what one coin would buy.[27] The bills were so worthless that the continental congress resolved "… that whosoever shall offer, demand, or receive … more of the said bills for any lands, houses, goods, wares, or merchandise than the nominal sums at which the same might be purchased of the same person with gold or silver, every such person ought to be deemed an enemy to the liberties of these Colonies and treated accordingly."[28] An earlier draft contained language to bar them from all trade in the colonies.

But you have to give our Founding Fathers credit; they learned from their mistakes. By 1786, Thomas Jefferson had a clear understanding of this whole process and was able to write, "It will be asked how will the two masses of Continental and of State money have cost the people of the United States 72 millions of dollars when they are to be redeemed now with about 6 million. I answer that the difference being 66 millions has been lost on the paper bills separately by the successive holders of them. Everyone through whose hands a bill passed, lost on that bill what it lost in value during the time it was in his hands. This was a real tax on him; and in this way the people of the United States actually contributed those millions of dollars during the war, and by a mode of taxation the most repressive of all because the most unequal of all."[29] At the time he wrote this, the nation was still reeling from the consequences of *fiat* money. George Washington wrote to James Warren that, "The wheels of government are clogged and we are descending into the vale of confusion and darkness."[30] Two years later, he wrote in a letter to Henry Knox, "If any person had told me that there would have been such formidable rebellion as exists, I would have thought him a bedlamite, a fit subject for a madhouse."[31] Of course, the average citizen was not as perceptive as Mr. Jefferson. Many peoples' sentiments were expressed by the lady who remarked, "What a shame it is that Congress should let the poor soldiers suffer when they have power to make just as much money as they choose."[32] Remember, not one in a million can diagnose the problem.

We can be grateful today that the majority of delegates who assembled in Philadelphia in the late 1780s were "one man in a million" types who understood the fraud inherent in *fiat* money. With the chaos from the worthless continentals still fresh in their minds, they were overwhelmingly adamant about slamming the door shut on all use of *fiat* money by the government. In the discussions during the continental congress to revise the Articles of Confederation, Oliver Ellsworth, the third chief justice of the Supreme Court told the delegates, "This is a favorable moment to shut and bar the door against paper money. The mischief of the various experiments which have been made are now fresh in the public mind and have excited the disgust of all the respectable parts of America."[33] George Mason said that he had a moral hatred for paper money and that it was founded on fraud and knavery. John Langdon, the delegate from New Hampshire, would rather have rejected the whole plan of the federation than grant the new government the power to issue *fiat* money. George Reed, the delegate from Delaware, likened *fiat* money to the mark of the beast in Revelation. If you can tolerate one more quote, consider what Thomas Paine, who was not a delegate, wrote in the same year. He was strongly opposed to *fiat* money, which he called counterfeiting by the state. He particularly abhorred legal tender laws that force people to accept counterfeited money and thought that if any member of Congress moved for such a law, he ought to be punished by death.[34] An interesting idea.

And thus, it came to pass that the power to emit bills of credit (paper receipts for use as money), which was given to the Federal Government by the Articles of Confederation, was struck from the new constitution by a 4 to 1 margin. That's an 80% majority. Article I, Section 8, Paragraphs 2 and 5 of the Constitution only gives Congress the authority to borrow money, to coin money, and to regulate the value thereof. Section 10 specifically prohibits the state from using *fiat* money, as well. Article I, Section 10, Paragraph 1, reads, "No state shall ... coin money, emit bills of credit [i.e., *fiat* money], ... [or] make anything but gold and silver coin a tender in payment of debts."

Those words were authored by Roger Sherman. He was the only man to sign all four historic documents (Continental Association of 1774, the Declaration of Independence, the Articles of Confederation, and the U. S. Constitution). He was well aware of the evil of *fiat* money and had even written a treatise against it. Jefferson said of him that he never spoke a foolish thing in his life. There is little doubt that if he had not stood up on that humid day in August 28, 1787 and uttered those words, the republic that had so recently defeated the British empire would have never gotten farther than a 5 year-old running away from home.[35] But in the providence of God, such was not the case. The tenth amendment adds one more nail to the coffin of *fiat* money. It specifically declares that the powers not given to the Federal Government are reserved to the people and the states. To those who can understand written English, that means you and I are the only ones that can print paper IOU's and use them as money.

America Defines Its Own Money

For a few years after this, we tried to use other people's money. But it did not take long before the need for our own system of money became apparent. The Spanish continued to devalue their dollar by using less and less silver in it. Eventually America was forced to coin its own money. After all, that was allowed by the Constitution.

Now before a nation can have its own money, there must be a system for measuring quantity. If concrete were to be used as money, it might measured in cubic yards; if gas were to be used, its quantity might be expressed in gallons; if lumber were to be used as money, its quantity might be expressed in board feet. But none of these commodities were options for use as money because the constitution specified that America would use gold and silver. The most logical system of units for measuring these commodities is weight. At the time, there were two systems of weight, the avoirdupois system, in which there are 16 ounces, or 7000 grains, to a pound and the troy system, in which there are 12 ounces, or 5760 grains, to a pound. But neither of these is practical for the measurement of precious metals. Most purchases require far less than one ounce of gold. It is also highly advantageous to put the commodity being used as money into a standard, easily distinguished form. If you went to Sears and asked the clerk how much a shirt costs, you would not want to hear 0.02 ounces of gold, 90% pure. You would then have to pull out your gold chunks and try to find some that added up to 0.02 ounces. It is just a little cumbersome. On the other hand, the clerk does not want to be concerned with the purity of your gold. You would both prefer to have a convenient unit to measure quantity and to have it exist in a known or recognizable form. The ability to determine both the unit of measure and the form and purity is what the constitution means when it speaks of the power to coin money and regulate the value thereof.

Using their constitutional power to coin money and regulate its value, Congress defined a new unit of weight, based on the troy system, that was both simple and convenient. They created a decimal system of weight using the units of dollars, dimes, cents (a cent being the hundredth part of a dollar), and mils (a mil being the thousandth part of a dollar). This means that the dollar is really a unit of weight like the pound and the ton and the ounce. The Mint Act, passed on April 2, 1792, decreed, "The money of account of the United States shall be expressed in dollars and cents"[36] and went on to define the dollar as a unit of weight equal to 371.25 grains if you were measuring pure silver. It provided for half-dollar, quarter-dollar, and dime weights of silver as well. Notice that these coins are not silver dimes or silver dollars. Strictly speaking, there is no such thing as a silver dime or silver dollar, just like there is no such thing as a water gallon or a water quart. You can have a gallon of water or a quart of water and you can have a dime of silver or a dollar of silver.

Although this use of the word dollar may seem strange, it is exactly how the Scriptures use the word shekel. In some places, it refers to a shekel as if it were a coin, whereas in other places, it obviously uses the word "shekel" as a unit of weight. In Exodus 30:13, we read that everyone must pay a tax of one-half shekel when they are numbered. In the New Testament, when Jesus sent Peter to retrieve a coin for the temple tax, it was a shekel that he pulled out of the mouth of the fish [Matthew 17:34]. But on the other hand, when Moses enumerated the offerings of the princes at the dedication of the tabernacle, he used the word "shekel" to describe the weight of the gold and silver gifts. One gift was a silver charger that weighed 130 shekels. Another gift was a gold gift weighing 10 shekels. Clearly, by saying that someone paid a shekel is meant that someone paid a gold or silver coin weighing one shekel.

Figure 4. Gold Coins of the United States. From the bottom: Twenty, Ten, Five, Two and a Half, and One Dollar Weights of Gold. The Sizes are Exactly Proportional to their Weights.

For some, distinguishing between a silver dollar and a dollar of silver is just semantics. Maybe it is. I think it is still an important distinction. You have to understand the words of a subject before you can really understand the subject. Language is not only a tool to communicate, it is also a weapon to mislead, to create wrong impressions, to induce false thinking. Word control is mind control, mind control is people control, and people control is totalitarian rule. The meaning of words is critical. Back to our gold.

In 1792, gold was considered to be 15 times more valuable than silver. In order to accommodate this difference in value, the Mint Act of 1792 set the dollar equal to 24.75 grains of gold. Ten dollars of gold weighed 247.5 grains. Thus, there were two weights claiming to be a dollar: 24.75 grains if one was using gold and 371.25 grains if one was weighing silver. Instead of fixing the weight and letting the relative value be determined in the market place, they tried to fix the relative value. But values can change and did change. This, I believe, was a well-intentioned mistake. It is equivalent to walking into a grocery store and seeing a 15-pound bag of salt that weighs 15 pounds and next to it a bag of sugar weighing one pound but marked as 15 pounds. When you ask the grocer why the "15 pound" bag of sugar does not weigh as much as the 15 pound bag of salt, he tells you, "Oh, don't you know sugar is 15 times more valuable than salt." It is sort of like having two weights in your bag, a large and a small. God forbids this in Deuteronomy 23:13 – 15. He says, "Thou shalt not have in thy bag divers weights, a great and a small. Thou shalt not have in thine house divers measures, a great and a small. [But] thou shalt have a perfect and just weight, a perfect and just measure shalt thou have: that thy days may be lengthened in the land which the LORD thy God giveth thee."

Having two weights leads to all types of confusion in the marketplace as you try to decide whether the bag of sugar or the bag of salt is the one which weighs 15 pounds. In this particular case, people were not defrauded by the duplicity of standards. They were not forced to use the gold or the silver. So if, as happened, gold becomes 16 or 18 times the value of silver, people could simply stop using the gold. For example, let us assume a suit cost $1. Because you like color variety in your money you have 1 dollar of gold in your left hand (weighing 24.75 grains) and, in your right hand, 1 dollar of silver that was 15 times as heavy (because silver was one fifteenth the value of gold). You know that you can go to the goldsmith and he will give you 20 dollars of silver for your dollar of gold. Which coin would you use to purchase the suit? Anyone with any sense will use the silver and keep the gold. That is exactly what happened. Professional economists call this bit of common sense Gresham's Law, after an official in Queen Elizabeth's court who first made the observation that bad money drives better money out of existence.[37]

The other thing the Mint Act of 1792 did was to make minting coins without the full amount of gold or silver a felony punishable by death.[38] There are many people walking around today who are glad this law is not being enforced.

This sound monetary policy was not without its critics, who clamored that there was not enough gold and silver for a rapidly growing economy. But they were soon shut up by the absolutely remarkable, hitherto unfathomable, growth. The Pennsylvania Gazette declared on December 16, 1789, barely a year after ratification, that, "Since the federal constitution has removed all danger of our having a paper tender, our trade has advanced 50%."[39] And that was just the beginning. Exports shot from $19 million in 1791 to $93 million in 1801. That's nearly 500% growth in 10 years. Today, we measure economic growth in tenths of a percent unless we are measuring the growth of the national debt. The deficit, which consumed 28% of the budget in 1792, was converted to a surplus as large as the budget by 1802. Today, the interest on our debt stands at about 15% of the national budget. Do you hear any sane person claiming we could pay off the national debt in 10 years? However, as we will see later, the national debt is, in a sense, only a figment of everyone's imagination.

What happened to slow this phenomenal growth? Although the constitutional convention slammed the door shut on paper money, it left the window open—they allowed the Federal Government to borrow money. This provided a way around the constitutional prohibition on paper money. The government chartered banks that issued the paper notes and gave them to the government. The net result is the same as if the government had itself printed the receipts. The debate over whether the nation should have a central bank consumed barrels of ink in the first part of the century. Had our ancestors remembered their history lessons better, they would not have so easily fallen prey to the same old lies and repeated the same banking mistakes.

But just as in the days of the Founding Fathers, we were blessed with another leader in the 1830s who both perceived what was really going on with the central bank and had the courage to stand for truth, even in the face of strong public opinion to the contrary. Andrew Jackson's courage in shutting down the central bank preserved this nation from the slavery of a fraudulent central bank for another 80 years. But the proponents of central banks were patient and, as the next chapter shows, in due time obtained all that they desired.

Chapter 5

The Founding of the Federal Reserve Corporation

A few years ago, the *St. Louis Globe Democrat* ran an article entitled, "Just What is Money, Does Anybody Know?" by Lewis Rukeyser.[40] It begins "Some of the nations leading experts on money have begun very quietly to make what many would regard as an astonishing admission: they do not know what they are talking about. In this case, as it happens, they mean it quite literally; they do not know what "money" is in 1982."[41] One of the economists interviewed for the article was a George W. McKinney Jr. He was a highly respected economist who would soon be retiring from the New York Irving Trust Company. Rukeyser asked him, " 'Is it then that we just don't know what money is these days?'

'Never did know,' confessed McKinney — and then, while listeners to our conversation chuckled nervously, made it clear he was not kidding." Irving Trust is no insignificant bank, and Mr. McKinney is no spring chicken. What would you think if you wrote a letter to Shell Oil and asked their chief chemist what gasoline was and he wrote back saying that he didn't know and never did know? Or maybe you write the President of the National Education Association and ask him what a good education should consist of and he wrote back, "Don't know and never did know." Come to think of it, I'd believe him. Even the *Wall Street Journal* remarked in a front page note on an upcoming IMF meeting, "a pre-IMF seminar of eminent economists could not agree on what "money" is or how banks create it."[42]

These incidents prove yet again the sad truth of Keynes' assertion that not one man in a million can understand or accept the process by which the currency is debauched. If these anecdotes are to be believed, then it is even worse than Keynes suggests. Apparently, the nations leading economists don't even know what money is. But it need not be so. A knowledge of history and a dictionary to tell us the simple meaning of words will go a long way in explaining the money mystery.

One of the earliest comprehensive explanations of the international banking network came in 1966 when Carroll Quigley published his magnum opus, *Tragedy and Hope*. It is a scholarly, 1300-page monster that some believe was never intended to be read by the masses.[43] It was written to an intellectual and political elite to whom he exposed many hitherto unrecorded details.

It should be noted that Dr. Quigley is a man of impeccable academic credentials. Former President William Clinton was his history student at Georgetown University and identified him as a mentor in his second acceptance speech of the democratic party nomination in 1995. Quigley authored a widely used history text and was a member of the editorial board of *Current History*, both of which indicate his acceptance and popularity in the academic community. He was a frequent lecturer and consultant for such groups as the Industrial College of the Armed Forces, the Brookings Institute, the US Naval Weapons Laboratory, the Naval College, the Smithsonian Institute, and the State Department. His resume has been detailed on these pages to emphasize the fact that Carroll Quigley was no quack, merely tolerated on the outskirts of academia. He was a respected scholar who commanded attention and prestige. According to his own testimony, he was personally acquainted with the super-rich family dynasties of whom he wrote and was a friendly apologist of their activities. He penned these words in *Tragedy and Hope*, "I know of the operation of this network [the banking network] because I have studied it for twenty years and was permitted for two years in the 1960's to examine its papers and secret records. I have no aversion to it or to most of its aims and have, for much of my life, been close to it and to many of its instruments [translate that as "people"]. I have objected both in the past and recently to a few of its policies … but in general my chief difference of opinion is that it wishes to remain unknown, and I believe its role in history is significant enough to be known."[44]

Clearly, Quigley is a credible witness. Not all of the authors that will be quoted will receive this level of detail, but most are equally distinguished and respected. On the basis of their testimony and in conjunction with the historical record, I believe that there is no longer much room for a reasonable person to doubt the goals and intents of the Federal Reserve Corporation. Nearly everything can be confirmed by at least two or three independent witnesses and often more. These words and writings of important men, combined with the world events of this century and particularly the last several years, leave no doubt about their veracity. You be the judge.

A Duck Hunt by the Seashore

As G. Edward Griffin has so melodramatically described in *The Creature From Jekyll Island,* the blueprints for the Federal Reserve Corporation were developed during a secret excursion to a very exclusive hunting resort off the coast of Brunswick, GA in November of 1910. Seven men, representing an estimated one sixth of the wealth of the entire world,[45] assembled in utmost secrecy at their own private island resort where they spent the next nine days planning a banking cartel that would eventually gain absolute control of this nations money. Who were these men and why did they take such great pains to disguise the nature of their visit? They were certainly not going duck hunting as they would have had the reporters assembled at Brunswick believe.

The owner of the private rail car that carried them to their destination and the organizer of the retreat was Nelson Aldrich, senator from Rhode Island. Aldrich was one of those rare men who wielded more power as a wealthy member of the international banking community than he did by virtue of being a senator. Griffin notes that "as an investment associate in the J. P. Morgan firm, he had extensive holdings in banking, manufacturing, and public utilities. His son-in-law was John D. Rockefeller, Jr. Sixty years later, his grandson, Nelson Aldrich Rockefeller, would be Vice-President of the United States."[46] The other members of the party were as follows:

Abraham Piatt Andrew	Assistant Secretary of the U.S. Treasury
Henry P. Davison	Senior partner of the J. P. Morgan Company
Charles D. Norton	President of J. P. Morgan's First National Bank
Benjamin Strong	Head of J. P. Morgan's Banker's Trust Company
Paul Warburg	Partner in Kuhn Loeb & Company and representative of the Rothschild banking dynasty.
Frank A. Vanderlip	President of the National City Bank and representative of Standard Oil and the Rockefeller fortune[47].

Many people have downplayed the significance and intent of this secret trip, labeling as simpletons those who think otherwise. However, twenty-five years later in an article for the *Saturday Evening Post*, Mr. Vanderlip himself penned these words:

> Despite my views about the value to society of greater publicity for the affairs of corporations, there was an occasion, near the close of 1910 when I was as secretive - indeed as furtive- as any conspirator. None of us who participated felt that we were conspirators; on the contrary we felt we were engaged in a patriotic work. We were trying to plan a mechanism that would correct the weaknesses of our banking system as revealed under the strains and pressures of the panic of 1907. I do not feel it is an exaggeration to speak of our secret expedition to Jekyll Island as the occasion of the actual conception of what eventually became the Federal Reserve System. [He then summarizes some of the preliminary events concerning the formation of a congressional monetary commission to visit Europe and study their central banks.]
>
> As the time for the assembling of Congress drew near, Senator Aldrich became increasingly concerned about the report he must write on behalf of the joint monetary commission; likewise, there ought to be, he knew, a bill to present to the new congress, and none had been drafted. This was how it happened that a group

> of us went to Jekyll Island Club on the coast of Georgia. Since it would be fatal to Senator Aldrich's plan to have it known that he was calling on help from Wall Street to help him in preparing his report and bill, precautions were taken that would have delighted the heart of James Stillman [a major stockholder in the Federal Reserve]. Those who had been asked to go were Henry Davison ... [see list above]. We were told to leave our names behind us. We were told further that we should avoid dining together on the night of our departure. We were instructed to come one at a time and as unobtrusively as possible to the railroad terminal on the New Jersey littoral of the Hudson, where Senator Aldrich's car would be in readiness, attached to the rear of a train bound for the South. When I came near the car the blinds were drawn and only slender threads of amber light showed the shape of the windows. Once on board the private car we began to use the taboo that had been fixed on last names. We addressed one another as "Ben,"... . Davison and I adopted even deeper disguises, abandoning even our first names. On the theory that we were always right, he became Wilbur and I became Orville ... The servants and the train crew may have known the identities of one or two of us, but they did not know all, and it was the names of all of us printed together that would have made our mysterious journey significant in Washington, in Wall Street, and even in London. Discovery, we knew, simply must not happen or else all our time and effort would be wasted. If it were to be exposed publicly that our particular group had gotten together and written a banking bill, that bill would have [had] no chance whatsoever of passage by Congress. ... Now although the Aldrich Federal Reserve Plan was defeated when it bore the name Aldrich, nevertheless its essential points were all contained in the plan that finally was adopted.[48]

Vanderlip went on to provide us with more detail concerning the purpose of the plan and its alleged benefit to humanity. Jesus comment, however, regarding evil deeds and darkness[49] was probably a more accurate description of their activity.

In the providence of God, the cozy relation between dishonest banking and the government had been mostly banished from this nation through the courage of Andrew Jackson during his presidency in the 1830s. The biggest goal of the seven businessmen on Jekyll Island was to reestablish this connection. These men wanted to implement in America what was already firmly entrenched in Europe, but had hitherto not been acceptable to the American people. They wanted a monopoly in which the government would authorize them to counterfeit and would use the power of the sword to keep others from doing the same. Their biggest challenge was to slip such a bill past Congress. Remembering that the best criminals are often the boldest, they packaged the whole plan as a bill to protect the public from banking fraud and to provide for an elastic money supply.[50]

Both of these were very tempting to the casual consumer of 1913. In those days, banking was not the tightly controlled monopoly that it is today. With a relatively small amount of initial capital or reserves, anyone could hang out their shingle and begin printing bank notes. Because it was so lucrative to loan money that didn't exist and then collect interest on it, many people did. Banking was growing so fast that the number of banks had doubled between 1900 and 1910. Many of these banks were nationally chartered and allowed to issue their own currency.[51] Figure 5 shows an example of this type of note.

As we saw earlier, along with these fraudulent notes comes the unavoidable cycle of booms and busts as the money supply expands and contracts in an unplanned and unexpected manner. Bank runs were routine occurrences. The people that participated in the fraud sometimes lost their shirt in the inevitable run on the bank. Thus, a bill to stop such losses sounded very good indeed.

And so, the birth of the Federal Reserve System came about in total secrecy during an alleged duck hunting trip to Jekyll Island. Even after their arrival at the remote island hunting lodge, they continued to use first names. They gave all of the regular staff a vacation for the entire nine days they were on the island. It was absolutely imperative that no one be able to recognize all of them. Represented among them were the world's leading banking firms, such as the Rothschild dynasty, the Warburgs, Kuhn Loeb, J. P. Morgan, and the Rockefellers. These men were actually competitors; to see them together would be a juicy news story that most reporters could not ignore, leading to many raised eyebrows and embarrassing questions. It would also doom any legislation if congress

Figure 5. Bank Note from Louisville, KY

found out that any of them had written the bill. Thus, the secrecy. Even the name was designed not to arouse people's fears about central banks by completely eliminating anything related to "central" or "bank" from the name. "Reserve" sounds much more assuring than bank — at least it did in that day. In former times, one used to frequently hear about people that did not trust banks. Personally, I always thought of them as being somewhat backward. But maybe they had just a bit more understanding we are willing to give them credit for.

During the next few years, Paul Warburg went to the people, to academia, and to Wall Street with a stream of speeches and pamphlets advocating and creating the need for an elastic money supply not tied to gold reserves and for a Federal Reserve to manage the money supply. Gold is scarce, he argued, and therefore hampered the development of commerce and industry. He reasoned that the unregulated independent banks that had proliferated in recent years were the cause of the panics and recessions and that a strong Federal Reserve was needed to bring the industry under control.

Warburg argued that an elastic money supply was necessary for a prosperous nation. We now have a very elastic money supply. If you want to build a house, you simply go to a bank and receive a loan. If you have a job and have not ruined your credit, it is nearly automatic. Even if everyone borrowed money tomorrow to build big shopping centers, bridges, and roads, the banks would still be able to loan everyone the money. They can do this without running out of money because of the elastic money supply in this nation. Exactly how it works will be explained shortly. But if the money supply were not elastic, then the banks could not give everyone a loan anymore than you could loan an indefinite amount of money to your children. Without an elastic money supply, it would be much harder to obtain a loan. There would only be so much money to go around, and no more. With an elastic money supply, the only limit on borrowing is the ability to handle the interest payments. Without an elastic money supply, borrowing is limited by both the availability of funds to loan as well as the cash flow of the borrower. This is a very real barrier which prevents the rampant borrowing so prevalent today.

Thus, when Warburg talked about an elastic money supply, one that could be expanded at will by the mere command of men, it looked as good to the sinful heart of greedy man as the forbidden fruit in the garden did to Eve. Our grandparents thought, and we have continued to believe, that they had outsmarted God and devised a way to avoid scarcity in their monetary resources. In believing that someone could expand the money supply at will, they believed that humans could speak money into existence. In believing that humans can create money from nothing, they believed a lie. Had our grandparents remembered the catechism they learned as children, they would have known that God alone can create. Man is only a steward of what God creates. We cannot create money any more than we can create apples. It makes no more sense to speak of an elastic money supply than it does to speak of an elastic apple supply. This deception is very similar to what happened in the Garden of Eden. The serpent, who was more crafty than any other beast, came to Eve and innocently asked her, "Yea, hath God said, Ye shall not eat of every tree of the garden?"

Eve replied that God had indeed said that, and what is more, He also said that they would die in the very day they ate of the fruit; Satan replied with his lie, "You surely shall not die." [Genesis 3:1,4] Eve believed the lie and mankind has been reaping the awful consequences of that deception ever since.

Warburg came to our grandparents with a similar question, "Has God said, 'All things were made by Him; and without Him was not any thing made that was made'?" Instead of laughing out loud in his face, they listened. Like Eve, they soon believed Warburg when he said that he could take a pile of money and expand it into a bigger pile simply by the stoke of his pen. In so doing, they believed a lie. We have been bearing the heavy tax of that deception ever since.

In a 1911 speech to the American Bankers' Association, Senator Aldrich said, "The organization proposed is not a bank, but a cooperative union of all the banks..." A little later he stressed that it would be nothing like the central bank that European nations had.[52] That does not say a whole lot about what the Act really was. Congressman Charles Augustus Lindberg Sr., the father of the famous aviator, was a little more descriptive. Speaking at great length on the floor of the house on the ill-fated night the legislation was passed, he said of the proposed legislation, "This Act establishes the most gigantic trust on earth such as the Sherman Anti-Trust Act would dissolve if Congress did not by this act expressly create what by that act it prohibited. When the President signs this Act, the invisible government by the money power, proven to exist by the money trust investigation, will be legalized"[53] In the same speech, he went on to say, "The new law will create inflation whenever the trusts want inflation. …The trust will soon realize they have gone too far even for their own good. This act places the jackscrew and the vice completely within their hands and the squeezing process, which they will apply to force the last bit of energy from the toilers to enrich the wealthy, will go to the point of maddening the people. … This bill empowers the banks to get more money from the credit of the people so as to collect more interest." In spite of these prophetic warnings, the bill passed the House in September and the Senate on December 19, 1913. There were over 40 major differences that had to be ironed out and Congressmen were assured that, as was customary, no action would be taken until the new year. But Monday, December 22, after some Congressmen and Senators had already left Washington, the New York Times ran the front-page headline "Money Bill May Be Law Today—Congress Had Adjusted Nearly All Differences By 1:30 This Morning."[54] All 40 differences were ironed out in one day, and the Federal Reserve Act was indeed passed into law that very day.[55] The true nature of this act began to appear over a year after its passage, when Senator Aldrich boasted, "Before the passage of this act, we could only dominate the reserves of New York. Now we are able to dominate the bank reserves of the entire country."[56] In case you are wondering exactly what bank reserves he is dominating, they are our deposits — in short, our money.

And, by the way, since this private corporation would be making staggering sums of money, it was exempted from all federal, state, and local taxes — everything, except real estate taxes.[57]

The Federal Reserve Act authorized a private corporation to print notes, called Federal Reserve Notes. One is pictured in Figure 6. It is a little bit bigger than the ones in use today, but otherwise, it looks like an ordinary ten-dollar bill. Now I have a question to ask you. "Is that bill pictured in Figure 6 ten dollars?" Let us find out.

A simple perusal of this piece of paper ought to reveal the answer. The first thing we see printed on it is a contract that says,

> The United States of America will pay to the bearer on demand ten dollars.

Figure 6 A. Front–Federal Reserve Note from 1914 Series

Figure 6 B. Back–Federal Reserve Note from 1914 Series

Consider this: if this is a contract to pay ten dollars, how can it be the 10 dollars it is promising to pay? Secondly, we note that the contract does not tell us what it is that we are to get ten dollars of. You have to turn it over and read the fine print to learn that important information. On the reverse side (See Figure 7) it reads,

> This note is receivable by all national and member banks, and federal reserve banks for all taxes, customs, and public debts.

Figure 7. Contract on the 1914 Series FRN

Notice that it says public debts. Everyone understood that the government cannot specify what you as an individual must take in payment of debt anymore than the government can specify what you offer for sale in your grocery store. This says nothing about anyone having to accept it for private debts. Why? The money of account of the United States at that time was specified by both the Mint Act of 1792 and Title 31 USC 371 to be gold and silver coin … period.[58] Nowhere does anyone presume to dictate what private persons must accept in payment of debt. The law only declares what government will accept in payment of debts. Notice that the only banks that must accept this note are national banks and Federal Reserve Banks. It would be unlawful to require state banks to accept them. Article 1, Section 10 of the US Constitution specifies that no state shall make anything but gold and silver coin a tender in payment of debts. The note goes on to say that it could be redeemed for gold by the bearer on demand or it could be redeemed for lawful money. What is lawful money? Well, lawful money was declared to be gold and silver coin. So you could redeem this note for ten dollars of gold or gold or silver coin. That is not ten dollars worth of gold but a ten dollar weight of gold. Ten dollars worth of gold does not mean anything. Worth is not an objective quantity. What is a comb worth to a bald man? What is a refrigerator worth to an Eskimo? How much would that same refrigerator be worth to a resident of Houston in July or August. What is the worth of ten dollars of gold to Robinson Crusoe? How much would ten dollars of gold be worth in your case? Who knows.

Even the fact that this bill contained a contract to pay a ten-dollar weight of gold may not have been apparent to our parents and grandparents because the contract was written in several different fonts with a picture of Jackson thrown in between. But the bigger problem is that the Federal Reserve was only required to back these notes with 40% gold and 100% eligible paper. What is eligible paper? Eligible paper is a short term IOU. What are IOUs? They are the things that my Dad used to give me when he needed to borrow from my piggy bank. He gave me a piece of paper that said I O U such and such. It is a promise to pay. What is a note? A note is absolute and unconditional promise by the maker to pay a specified sum of money to someone at a specified time. So a note is a promise to pay. Now tell me truly; can you "redeem" this promise to pay with another promise to pay just like it? What would you think if a circus gave away free admission tickets to all the children in a certain school class that said, "General Admission, Admit Four to the Barnum Brothers Circus, Main Show, anywhere in the US during the 1913 – 1914 season." When you took your family of four to the circus in your city, and presented the ticket for admission, the ticket master said, "What would you prefer, 4 tickets that admit one person, or 2 tickets that admit 2 people each?" You would either think his trapeze didn't return all the way or that you were the victim of a bad joke. What if you paid three hours of labor for those tickets? But when the Federal Reserve does the same thing, we stand in awe of their brilliance and work even harder to obtain their IOU notes. We believe everything is okay as long as we can pass the bogus circus coupons around among our friends (or enemies) and receive goods and services for them, even though we know the circus master will never let us into the circus with them.

Chapter 6

The *Faith Money* of the Federal Reserve Corporation

This analysis only raises another question. If the Federal Reserve Corporation was only required to back these notes with 40% gold and 100% eligible paper, did the notes have 140% backing? No, they had only 40% backing. Right from the beginning they were 60% fraud and 100% theft in favor of the issuer. Who was the issuer? The Federal Reserve Corporation. Now what would you think if an airline sold 100 tickets for a flight to Orlando, Fl in January. That is a nice place to go in the winter. You buy a ticket and go to the gate at the appropriate time. After 40 people get on, the attendant tells you that the plane is full. Being one of the 60, you go back to the counter and tell the attendant you want a refund, there was no seat on the plane for you.

"That's right," the attendant says, "We only have 40 seat airplanes. I can't refund any money because you have a non-refundable ticket. We are authorized by law to do that you know."

"I see," you reply thoughtfully, "By the way, how's business?"

"Just great," he says with a big smile.

That is essentially what Congress authorized a private corporation called the Federal Reserve to do in when it passed the Federal Reserve Act of 1913. But this is just the tip of the proverbial iceberg. At that time, people could still go to a bank and redeem these IOUs for gold coin. At least 40% of the people could. Although the contract was not as clearly stated on the Federal Reserve Notes as it was on the National Currency issues prior to the Federal Reserve Act, people could still circulate gold. Whoever holds the gold, makes the rules. The people of the United States still held gold, and government was still by the consent of the governed. If totalitarian power was to be gathered into the hands of these bankers, then this would have to change. The fact that gold was the lawful money of account in this land, and the fact that it had once circulated, had to be sunk into the collective memory hole of the American people; never to be remembered again, until such time as it could be safely resurrected as a historical relic of no modern significance. In pursuit of this goal, the portions of the mint act that allowed people to bring gold to the mint and have it coined were repealed in 1934. Also revoked in the same legislation was the ability of American citizens to own gold bullion.

Following this legislation, a new series of Federal Reserve Notes was issued. These notes had the same contract: "The United States of America will pay to the bearer on demand ten dollars." (See Figure 8.) But the fine print to the left, which told us what we were to get ten dollars of, had been changed. It now read,

> This note is legal tender for all debts public and private and is redeemable in lawful money at the United States Treasury or and Federal Reserve Bank.

This note claims to be legal tender. What is that? Legal, according to Black's Dictionary, 5th Edition, means the form of law. Lawful, on the other hand, contemplates the substance of law. It is legal in this country to murder unborn children because the form of law — a bill passed by Congress or a Supreme Court Opinion — allows it. But it is not lawful and never will be lawful to murder unborn children. The substance of law — the words that proceed from the mouth of the Lord — forbids it. This note is claiming to be legal; that is, according to the form of law or formal. It also claims to be tender. Tender is a verb meaning to offer. So this note is a formalistic offer to pay all debts public and private and is redeemable in lawful money. So once again we ask, if this note is a formalistic offer to pay and is redeemable in lawful money, can it, itself be lawful money? I do not think so. The promise to pay is not the same as the payment. When you offer this note to someone you are giving them

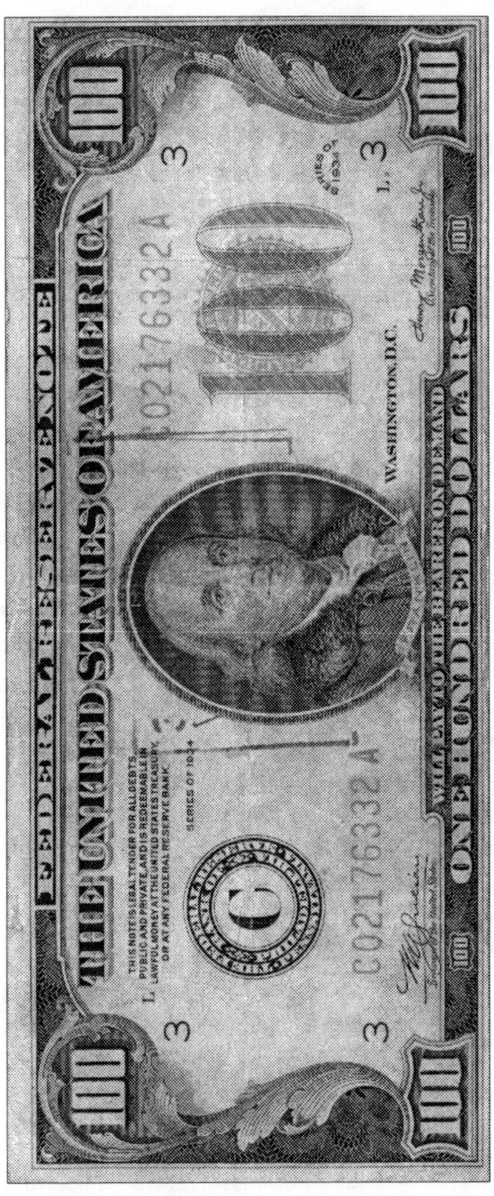

Figure 8. Series 1934 Federal Reserve Note

an IOU. You are giving them a piece of paper that is the promise or offer to pay the debt at some future date. The debt can only be paid by the bearer taking this IOU back to the person that issued it and demanding a redemption. Payment only occurs when the note is redeemed by the issuer. Can this note be redeemed in lawful money? What is the lawful money that you would get if you redeemed it? 12 USC 152 says that gold or silver coin of the US shall be construed to be the lawful money of the United States. But American citizens could not own any gold. That only left silver as lawful money.

In 1945, the reserve requirement was dropped to 25%. In 1950 the Federal Reserve made some cosmetic adjustments to their note. The four lines of large print on the left were changed into three lines of small print. Why did they do that? Were they trying to cut printing costs on these notes? Were they trying to save ink? Hardly. Or was it psychological preparation for what they ultimately did one day in 1963, when the American people were burying their slain leader? On that day in November, the Federal Reserve Corporation issued a new set of notes that looked very much like the old ones. The contract read,

The United States of America … ten dollars.

OOPS! Where did the 'will pay to the bearer on demand' phrase go? Are they suggesting that this piece of paper **is** ten dollars? Does the removal of the promise to pay a ten-dollar weight of gold convert this piece of paper into the ten dollars that it was promising to pay? Of course not. Looking on the left of the new notes, we can now understand why the four lines of large print had been changed to three lines of small print in 1950. In place of the three lines of small print are two lines of large print which read simply, "This note is legal tender for all debts public and private." These two lines of large print are about the same size as the three lines of small print. There is nothing said about anything being redeemable in anything anymore. This statement has remained unchanged to this day.

If you still think that a dollar is a piece of paper, then let me ask you another question. If a tuna was a fish, wouldn't 50 tuna have to be 50 fish? If some piece of paper was a dollar, wouldn't 50 dollars have to be 50 pieces of paper? Of course they would. This piece of paper is like the deed to your property. The size of the deed has nothing to do with the size of your property because the deed to your property is not the same as the property. The deed to 1 acre is exactly the same size as the deed to 1000 acres. In summary, removing the promise to pay does not convert the piece of paper containing the promise to pay into the substance that it promised to pay.

Let us look again at this note. It claims to be a Federal Reserve Note. Is it? First of all, is it Federal? Does it have anything to do with the Federal Government. If you look on page 13 of their publication, *The Hats the Federal Reserve Wears*, they say that the federal reserve is not a part of the government.[59] If you write to the Federal Reserve asking for some of their publications, they will send them to you free and even take care of the postage. If you look in the upper right hand corner of the envelope you will find a Pitney Bowes meter stamp just like every other corporation in the United States uses. There is no government eagle franking their mail. They also have a corporate seal and will tell you the date that they were incorporated, and it was not July 4, 1776 or any other date around that time, but rather December 23, 1913. Lastly, if you want to give these folks a call, they are located in the white pages along with every other non-government entity. Or, if you prefer the direct approach, look in the Federal Reserve Act itself. There we read that the Federal Reserve is a corporation that has legal standing to both sue and defend itself from lawsuit in court.[60] So this paper is not Federal at all in the sense of having to do with the Federal Government.

The next word is "reserve." Reserves are funds on hand to redeem a negotiable instrument such as a check or a note. There are no funds on hand to redeem this note. There is no place that one can go to obtain a dollar weight of any substance, let alone gold or silver, and thereby redeem the note. In *Coins and Currency*, by the New York Federal Reserve Bank, we are told that as of 1968 there are no longer any reserve requirements.[61] In *I Bet You Thought*, the same bank tells us that currency notes cannot be redeemed or exchanged for treasury gold or any other assets used as backing. Didn't they just admit that they pass worthless instruments at law? This piece of paper has nothing to do with reserves in any form, and in reality it never did.

It is also claiming to be a "note." What is a note? A note is an absolute and unconditional promise by someone to pay someone a specified amount at a specified time. Is there any such promise here? It does not say who is paying, to whom anything is to be paid, what is to be paid, or when it is to be paid. It is not even a note. The older series could at least claim to be a note.

It says that it is ten dollars, as if a dollar was an entity like a apple or nail instead of a unit of weight equal to 24.75 grains of gold. But it is not ten dollars. It is only one piece of paper. How can it be ten of anything? How can a piece of paper be gold weighing 247.5 grains of fine gold. So this is not ten dollars.

This piece of paper also claims to be legal tender. Notice that it does not claim to be cash, currency, or money. It is not cash, it is not currency, and it is not even a note.

Is it legal tender? We said that legal tender was a formalistic offer to pay.

Does it offer to pay? No.

Will it pay the money at par? No.

This is not Federal, has nothing to do with reserves, it is not a note, it is not ten dollars, and it is not legal tender. This is a five-way fraud just on the face of it. Removing the promise to pay does not convert this paper into the ten dollars that it promised to pay. If it could, then a promise to pay a hat would be a hat. Therefore, the courts have ruled that this is abandoned tender. Maybe you have written a ten-dollar check when you only had five dollars in your account and inadvertently abandoned your tender. Was your check half good? No. It was a bad check because you have abandoned your tender or offer to pay the ten dollars. Abandoned tender cannot be legal tender.

What are we going to call these pieces of paper? I'll suggest a term: Trojan dollars. They are fancy drawings, spent into the economy and eagerly received, that soon bring financial disaster on the unfortunate recipients and enormous wealth to the issuers

Maybe you are saying, yes, but I can go down to the grocery store and obtain all the food I need with these pieces of paper, whatever you want to call them. How can they be so bad?

First, nobody denies that they have utility. For example suppose Local Grocer has a nice basket of fruit for $20 that Loyal Customer wants to buy.

"Mr. Grocer," Loyal Customer asks, "Will you take a check from me made out to cash?"

"Sure," he says, "I'll take a check from you from a loyal customer."

Mr. Customer takes his fruit basket and gives Local Grocer the check. Later, Local Grocer goes across the street to Mr. Gas Station and asks Gas if he will accept a check from Loyal Customer for some gas. Knowing Loyal Customer, Gas Station agrees to accept the check in exchange for his gas. The next day he goes to the flower shop and buys flowers with Loyal Customer's check; the flower shop proprietor then takes the check to the bank. But when he tries to deposit it, the banker informs him that the check is no good as Loyal Customer closed out that account a few weeks ago. In this example, who was defrauded? The man who tried to redeem the check. He was out $20. It was a 100% loss. But what about Loyal Customer? He gained $20 with no labor. He received the basket of fruit for nothing while the flower shop proprietor received nothing for his flowers. Although no one in-between paid anything, they were all compensated. The fact that people gave up the fruit of their labor in exchange for the bad check and were compensated in later transactions does nothing to change the fact that it was a bad check. It does not matter if someone gave up the moon for the check or if the check circulates for years — it is still a bad check. The first person obtains something for nothing and the last person to negotiate the check will get nothing for something.[62] No one is paid until the issuer redeems it at par. The only reason that the check traded was because people trusted the issuer, Loyal Customer. The only reason people accept these Trojan dollars in exchange for their labor is their *faith* that others will also accept them — and our belief that our own government would not perpetrate a fiscal fraud upon us.

What! Faith-based money? Yes. Even the Federal Reserve Corporation agrees, saying, "Faith in the strength, soundness, and stability of the American economy is the real backing of our money."[63] What is happening to that trust today? It is slipping. What happens when it is all gone? The same thing that always happens when people lose faith in their bank. They show up to get their money out. But where are people going to go to get their money today? Have you seen a Federal Reserve Bank lately? Will people know where it is, or what it is, or even who it is that is responsible for the mess they are in? No. Instead, the crowds will simply mill around the streets not sure upon whom to vent their frustration. Another name for this is rioting. As the 2001 World Trade meetings in Seattle illustrate, riots are becoming all too frequent even in America.

Federal reserve notes are an attempt to get what you produce and never pay. Any note, legitimate or illegitimate, is an attempt to get your produce now without payment. A legitimate note is an attempt to get what you produce now and pay you later. An illegitimate note is an attempt to get what you produce now and pay you never. The respected Hoover Institute scholar, Anthony Sutton had this to say about the Federal Reserve,

> Warburg's revolutionary plan to get American Society to go to work for Wall Street was astonishingly simple. Even today academic theoreticians cover their blackboards with meaningless equations and the general public struggles in bewildered confusion with inflation and the coming credit collapse, while the quite simple explanation of the problem goes undisclosed and almost entirely uncomprehended. The Federal Reserve is a legal private monopoly of the money supply operated for the benefit of the few under the guise of protecting and promoting the public interest.[64]

The mechanism by which all this occurs is as interesting as it is absurd. When the smoke and mirrors are removed, it is really very simple. We will discover a situation that is not all that different from the type of illusions created by the Wizard of Oz which Toto the dog revealed when he pulled back the curtain. The only problem is that Toto has not yet arrived.

Where Do Banks Get Whatever It Is That They Loan?

If you are like I used to be, you probably think that banks accept deposits from people who have money and then loan those deposits out to others needing the money. But apparently, that is not what we do today. According to the monetary authority of the United States, in *Modern Money Mechanics,* they say, "Banks can build up deposits by increasing loans and investments."[65] Now I am a simple fellow. I know what deposits are: they are the piles behind the barn. If my neighbor comes over to borrow some deposits, the pile gets smaller. I think most children could figure out that when you loan something, you, the lender, have less of whatever it is that you loaned. But the Federal Reserve is saying that they can increase their deposits by loaning. They must not be loaning deposits. They are actually loaning the promise to pay or an IOU. They simply tell the borrower that they will honor his checks for $1000 over the amount currently on deposit. This is not my analysis. *Modern Money Mechanics* says, "Of course they [banks] do not really pay out loans from the money they receive as deposits. If they did this, no additional money would be created. What they do when they make loans is to accept promissory notes in exchange for credits to the borrower's "transaction account"[66] — that is what they call your checking account. Later they reiterate, "Loans are made by crediting the borrower's deposit account, i.e., by creating additional deposit money."[67] What is a credit to your checking account? A book entry made with their pen or their computer. They do not even give you an IOU or note which is a promise to pay.[68] Of course the irony of it all is that it is your integrity that is questioned when you apply for a loan. No one ever thought to question their integrity.

Debt, as opposed to salt, tobacco, or gold, is being used as money. In essence, debt has been "monetized." Commercial banks are one of the ways debt is monetized. For example, suppose you come to a commercial banker for a loan of $1000 to build an outhouse with two electrically heated seats. The banker agrees to grant you a loan at 10% annual interest. In making this loan, he does not actually loan you any commodity — any money. He does not even loan you any Federal Reserve Notes. He simply makes a book entry with his pen — or nowadays with his computer. There is nothing that is loaned; no tangible substance changes hands. The banker simply increases the total on your account by $1000 and authorizes you to write checks against this increased total. In effect you print your own money as you write the checks. As a result of this transaction, the money supply is expanded by $1000, which as we saw earlier, causes inflation. You then find a carpenter willing to build this outhouse with the sweat of his brow, as Scripture commands, in exchange for your check or Federal Reserve Notes. In the meantime you begin to earn back the $1000 by the sweat of your brow just as Scripture commands. Finally, after a year, you have earned back the $1000 principle plus the $100 interest. You go back to the bank with the eleven worn 100-dollar bills that you have been saving, give them to the banker, and immediately feel like celebrating. (You want to celebrate because you were a slave the whole time you were in debt, but now you are free. Scripture says that the borrower is a servant of the lender.) While you are walking away feeling like a free man, what do you suppose the banker does with the $1100 you just placed in his hand? Eleven hundred dollars that the banker did not earn by the sweat of his brow, $1100 which he did not have before you came into my bank to borrow it, and therefore, $1100 that is not lawfully his. The paper that he now holds in his hand represents the labor of other people which he has obtained without any work or payment whatsoever. Does he just tear them up? Of course not. Instead, he goes to the same carpenter and asks him to build an outhouse just like yours — the one with two electrically heated seats. When the carpenter agrees to do it for $1100, the banker simply hands him the same notes you handed the banker. He gets for free what everyone else has to work for. No wonder banks are the biggest, most beautiful skyscrapers in town.

In actuality, paying back a debt extinguishes money in the exact opposite way that the act of loaning created money. Thus, the principle is not able to be spent as I have suggested. That would be too inflationary. However, the interest can be directly spent by the loaning bank. After ten loans, the bank has made an amount equal to the original principle. The point is that in receiving interest on money that did not exist prior to the loan, the bank can obtain money without labor. That is very different than receiving interest on money that has been earned by the sweat of one's brow as Scripture commands.

If a banker gets something for nothing, then someone else must be getting nothing for something. If he gets you to trust in his bad IOUs, then he does not have to work for them because you will. If you could write an IOU and get other people to trust it so much that they were willing to accept it in exchange for their labor, then you would not have to work either. His biggest challenge in doing this is to inspire confidence in his IOUs. Remember how the bad check writer got for free what other people had to work for? We called him a criminal. There is absolutely no difference between what the bank has done and what our bad check writer did. They both obtained for free what others had to pay for. They both obtained the labor of others without any labor on their part. That, folks, is theft — legalized theft. In a land where it is legal to murder unborn children, legal in most states to commit adultery, sodomy, and bestiality, legal to blaspheme the name of God, legal to break the Sabbath, legal to covet the possessions of others via lawsuits, and illegal to spank children for dishonoring their parents, is it any surprise to find that theft by certain people is also legal?

Is There A Limit To How Much Banks Can Loan?

In case you are wondering, there is a limit to the amount of money a bank can create. It is called the reserve requirement. The amount of loans that a bank can make is limited by the requirement to keep on deposit with the Federal Reserve Bank a certain percentage of their deposits. For example, let us assume that a bank receives a $10,000 deposit. If the reserve requirement is 10%, then the bank has to retain 10% of this deposit as reserves. It then has 9000 dollars called excess reserve which it can loan out. This money is loaned out and becomes deposits in other banks. These other banks keep 10% on reserve and loan out the excess - the other 90%. Eventually, the total deposits on record could theoretically reach ten times the initial deposit of $10,000. [See Appendix 1 if you want to see the math behind this]. In other words, the $10,000 has been multiplied to $100,000.[69] What is confusing is the fact that the deposits (which are just book entries) of one bank, are actually the loans of other banks or even their own loans.

Who collects interest on this money all the time? The bank.

Did they do any work to earn whatever it is that they loan? No. They only made entries in a book.

This is why large banks are willing to make mind-boggling loans to unstable third world countries and then refinance the debt, when they default, with even bigger loans. They are not loaning hard earned money. Rather, they are *interested* in the *interest* payments on the capital — capital that didn't exist until they loaned it.

If this seems hard to believe, consider this exchange recorded in the congressional record:[70]

Mr. Patman: Governor Eccles, when did the Federal Reserve bank first commence charging the government agencies a service charge for the services performed by the Federal Reserve bank?

Mr. Eccles: I really could not tell you. …

Mr. Patman: Wasn't it contemplated when the act [i.e., The Federal Reserve Act] was passed that the Federal Reserve bank would render this service without charge? …

Mr. Eccles: I would not think so. That would not be possible. The income of the Federal Reserve System would not be sufficient.

Mr. Patman: You could buy an unlimited amount of bonds by creating the money to buy them, could you not, and receive interest on those bonds?

Mr. Eccles: That is right.

Mr. Patman: Do you not get practically all your income from that source now.

Mr. Eccles: Yes.

Who needs printing presses to print receipts to loan, when people will accept your "promise to pay" as the loan and create the money in their head themselves. You can also see how assets have become confused with debts, and deposits are confused with loans, so that it is impossible to separate them in the banking system. The purpose of the Federal Reserve in this process is to enforce the same reserve requirement on everyone. If one bank had a high reserve requirement and one bank had a low one, the bank with a low reserve would always be out of money. There would be more checks cashed against their reserves than they had checks being deposited to their reserves. If I have a 50 % reserve, I have only committed to honor checks whose total can be twice the amount of money I have on deposit. On the other hand, with a 10% reserve requirement, I have given my word to honor checks totaling ten times the money on reserve. If I am at 10% while everyone else is at 50%, it is much more likely that I will not be able to honor all checks that are presented to me. This is called a currency drain; it used to be called a run on the bank. By enforcing the same reserve requirement, and loaning money to banks to make up any temporary shortfall [this is called the float], the Federal Reserve keeps everything in balance. That is why they are the check clearing house. By adjusting the reserve requirement, they can directly control the maximum amount of money available for circulation. This is a direct, but slow-acting control knob. They can also control the amount of money in circulation by controlling the interest rate. This is an indirect, but much faster-acting control knob. As the interest rate goes up, people will borrow less. When people borrow less, there is less multiplication of money through the fractional reserve process. When interest rates are down, people borrow more, causing greater multiplication of money. In this way, the Federal Reserve Corporation can manipulate the economy at will. They can effect changes in the unemployment rate, they can change the inflation rate, or any other rate. The effect of their policies are felt by everyone, everyday, in every way and yet you have not elected even one of these men. In fact, most people do not even know who they are.[71]

The next time you need money, try loaning some money instead of borrowing it. It works for the banks.

The Federal Government's Best Friend

The same process that goes on when an individual borrows money from a commercial bank goes on between the Federal Reserve and the Federal Government. The result is called the national debt. The Federal Reserve takes all of the government treasury bills that other investors do not buy and writes a check to the US Treasury for them. Is there any money to cover this check? No, but who will know. The Federal Reserve is the corporation that clears checks. They simply credit their asset side with the securities the US Treasury gave them and add to the liability side of their books the check they gave the government. Anyone else doing this would be sent to jail, but Congress allows the Federal Reserve to do this because it wants money, and this is a very convenient way to get it. Much more convenient than taxing the people. This is exactly equivalent to the Federal Reserve buying your house for $450,000 and writing you a check drawn on themselves. When you call the bank to verify sufficient funds, who do you get? The very person that gave you the check. Of course the check is good they tell you. You deposit it and the bank sends it to the issuing bank for payment. But the issuing bank is also the check clearing house. They are the ones that receive all checks and debit or credit other accounts accordingly. Of course the check clears the "bank." Who is any wiser? They credit the reserve account of your bank + $450,000 and your bank credits your account $450,000. After all, it is only computer blips that are being passed around. You now think you are half a million dollars richer, while the bank owns a nice home with out one minute of labor. (Of course the money supply has been increased by $450,000 and we know what effect that will have on the economy!)

In this case, the Federal Reserve is buying treasury bills from the Federal Government. They used to be a piece of paper on which the Federal Government promised to pay the bearer a sum of money. Since 1986, all government securities, except savings bonds, only exist in electronic form; i.e., a voltage in a computer.[72] The government deposits this check in a Federal Reserve Bank and proceeds to write their own checks against their account which we, in turn, accept in exchange for our labor. This is the second way that money is created. Every week, when the Federal Government auctions off its treasury bills, it is creating money. Although the government is now in debt, through that debt, it can obtain for free all the produce of our labor that it wants (or all that we are willing to give them). If the government is getting something for free, someone else must be getting nothing in exchange for their labor. That someone is you and me. The money that the government received is then paid out and deposited in commercial banks all around the country. It becomes the deposits from which banks can then create even more money—or even more debt depending on your perspective..

The National Debt—A Problem Or A Blessing?

This poses an interesting question: Is the national debt a problem or a blessing? You probably are thinking that I am going to tell you that the national debt is bad and we ought to get rid of it. Well, maybe it is. But we would have a rather interesting problem if we got rid of all debt including the national debt. *For if there was no longer any debt, either public or private, we would no longer have any money.* That's right! If all debt were paid off, there would be absolutely no money in circulation; everyone's bank account would be *zero!* Every dollar that is in circulation, every penny in circulation, has come into circulation by being borrowed. Did you know that you spend debt? You do not have to take my word for it. If you are having a hard time believing this from me, let me quote a few authorities. On September 30, 1941 the House Committee on Banking and Currency was in the process of gathering testimony on a bill that would have provided for Government ownership of the 12 Federal Reserve banks.[73] One of the people asked to testify was Marriner Eccles,

Governor of the Federal Reserve System at the time. He was engaged in the following dialog by Wright Patman, a young Texas representative and later committee chairman.

Mr. Patman: Do you believe that people should pay their debts generally when they can?

Mr. Eccles: I think that depends a good deal on the individual; but of course, **if there was no debt in our money system - there would not be any money.** [emphasis added]

Mr. Patman: Suppose everyone paid their debts, would we have any money to do business on?

Mr. Eccles: That is correct. [i.e., No, there would not be any money on which to do business.]

Mr. Patman: In other words our system is based entirely on debt.

The governor's reply, although quite fallacious, removes any vestige of doubt about the relationship of debt to our money system: "That is not our system alone, that is the capitalistic system."[74]

A little later in the testimony, Patman extracted another astonishing admission about the true nature of our money system.

Mr. Patman: The stock [of the Federal Reserve] amounts to almost nothing compared to the business of the Federal Reserve Banks. The stock is worth less than 140 million and you do several hundred billion dollars worth of business in a year, and you actually hold and claim now over two billion dollars in government securities which you claim you bought. How did you get the money to buy those two billion dollars of government securities?

Mr. Eccles: We created it.

You can almost hear the incredulity in Patman's reply.

Mr. Patman: Out of what?

Mr. Eccles: Out of the right to issue credit money.

You can almost hear the sarcasm in Mr. Eccles' voice. Here is a member of the House banking committee asking how the United States gets money. But Patman boldly pursued it a step further asking "There is nothing behind it, is there, except our government's credit?[75] After a partially successful attempt to evade the force of the question, the governor of the Federal Reserve conceded that our money system was debt.

Perhaps you prefer another source.[76] The Federal Reserve Bank of Chicago writes in *The Two Faces of Debt*, "...the Federal government through the Federal Reserve system issues non interest bearing debt — currency or paper money." [We have already shown that there is no such thing as paper money. Paper is far too heavy to use as money.] They go on. "Currency is so widely accepted ... that most people do not think of it as debt. Technically however, Federal Reserve Notes are liabilities."[77]

What are these little pieces of paper? Most people think of them as assets, but that is not what they are saying. No, the Federal Reserve Bank of Chicago, which is the monetary authority of the United States, as well as the issuer of these notes, is telling us they are debts. "Everyone knows what debt is when he owes it, but sometimes people forget that the assets they are trying to collect are actually other people's debts."[78] Did you know that? The assets you work so hard for, and look forward to receiving twice each month are actually the debts of others? Did you know assets are debts? That is what the Federal Reserve Bank of Chicago says: Debts are assets.[79] This process of converting debts into assets to be used as money is euphemistically called "monetizing" the debt.'

> If there was no debt, either national or private,
> there would be no money.

What is debt? We have been using the term: we should define it. Debt, according to Noah Webster (1828) is a sum of money due or a sum of money that is owed. [He also called it a vice or misfortune.] What are we using as money? A sum of money that is owed or sum of money due. Can you use a sum of money that is owed as money? Can you walk into a restaurant and eat a steak that is owed to the restaurant? Can you check out a book from the library that is due back at the library? Can you pay off a debt with more debt? To pay means to deliver money or the equivalent, whether it is property or goods or services, to someone. Payment is the delivery of money so that it is no longer owed. But we are using a sum of money owed as money. Can you deliver a sum of money owed in payment of a sum of money that is owed (debt)? If you do deliver it, is it still owed? Call for the logicians —wait, magicians might be a better choice — and tell them that we have a problem. The Tower of Babel project was disbanded because of a communication problem. We have no less of a confusion of language here. Language is being used to conceal and deceive. Returning to a strict construction of words would go a long way to exposing this fraud.[80]

The real function of the Federal Reserve is to convert debt into money. At least they try. But they cannot do it without us. We are a vital link in this process. Nobody can convert a pile of gold that does not exist, or is owed, into an asset unless we are willing to play along with the delusion. We must be willing to believe their lie and imagine that they have created money out of debt. When we do, we are exactly like the people who pretended that the naked emperor was actually wearing clothes. The creation of money really goes on in our heads when we trust in the Federal Reserve and the Federal Government and believe their deception. In a very real way, the federal deficit is a figment our imagination. The pieces of paper that we pass around, which I have called Trojan dollars, exist only to help maintain our confidence in the whole illusion. They serve as the curtains that surround the Wizard of Oz. Except in this case, no Toto has yet been able to pull back the curtains and expose the fraud for what it is. This deception is a spiritual problem. It is our judgment as a nation for having rejected God as our Creator and, therefore, our Lawgiver.

Do Banks Really Need To Charge Interest?

If the banks counterfeit every dollar that they loan and the Federal Government can obtain our labor and its produce without taxes, then why do banks charge interest and why does the government tax us? To answer, let us go back to our example of a bank loan for $1000 and consider the interest. If all money is created through loans, then where is the interest money going to come from so that the loan can be paid back with interest? If the bankers do not put the money into circulation, then it is not available for us to earn. I am speaking collectively of the nation as a whole. Sure, you as an individual can earn back the capital and interest to pay off your loan, but the nation as a whole cannot. The only money that exists is the principle of some debt. The only way to obtain this interest money is to work for the bank that loaned it. Again, I am speaking collectively. You can earn money from others to pay your loan off with interest. But collectively, the nation as a whole cannot unless they work for the bank. This is admitted by the Federal Reserve in *Two Faces of Debt*. There we read, "Debt is here to stay. The amount of debt will continue to grow. Existing debt will be refinanced over and over again."[81] If every dollar we hold is borrowed from the Federal Reserve which created it out of nothing and exchanged it for the produce of our labor, then what we have is nothing less than perpetual servitude. Collectively, we will never get out of debt. We cannot pay our debts unless the Federal Reserve puts the money into circulation for us to pay the interest. But every dollar that they put into circulation is another debt that will have to be paid off. This is perpetual servitude — they are the absolute masters and we are the absolute slaves.

It is also wickedness. God's word tells us that the wicked borrows and does not repay (Psalm 37:21). Perpetual debt is borrowing without repayment. In admitting that the debt created by their notes will never be repaid, the Federal Reserve Corporation is admitting perpetual wickedness.

The answer to our question about interest and taxes is that these are necessary to keep up the fraud. As long as we think that the Federal Government lives off our income tax and banks loan the deposits that we bring them, the fraud will be perpetrated from generation to generation. We will never understand why it is that although we make more and more money, we seem to have less and less, and why it is that cars gets more and more expensive, and why it is that more and more people are unable to work one job their whole life without getting laid off due to corporate failure, why it is that fewer and fewer newly weds can afford to buy a home, why we are becoming a debtor nation, and why the federal deficit seems to go higher and higher. All we know is that "I owe, I owe, its off to work I go." Never do we stop to contemplate who exactly is benefiting from all our labor.

Chapter 7

Economic Laws and Promises From Our Savior King

Some might be thinking at this point, "Well okay, Federal Reserve Notes might be fraudulent, but they are not really hurting anyone. As long as everyone keeps the faith, there is no real problem."

Are there any consequences beyond the tax of inflation? Does Scripture have an answer for this question?

Scripture actually has a great deal to say about the source of economic prosperity. When the children of Israel were preparing to enter the promised land, Moses recounted for them the history lessons that they had learned over the previous 40 years. In Deuteronomy 8, after reciting some of the economic blessings God had sent to them, such as the free food and the shoes that did not wear out, we read:

> Therefore you shall keep the commandments of the Lord thy God to walk in his ways, and to fear him. For the Lord thy God brings thee into a good land, a land of brooks of water, of fountains and depths that spring out of valleys and hills; A land of wheat and barley and vines and fig tress and pomegranates; a land of oil, olive, and honey; A land wherein thou shalt eat bread without scarceness, thou shalt not lack anything in it; a land whose stones are iron, and out of whose hills thou may dig brass.

When thou have eaten and are full, then thou shalt bless the Lord thy God for the good land which He hath given thee. Beware that thou forget not the Lord thy God in not keeping His commandments, and His judgments, which I command thee this day: Lest when thou have eaten and are full, and have built goodly houses and dwelt therein; and when thy herds and thy flocks multiply, and thy silver and thy gold is multiplied and all that thou have is multiplied; Then thine heart be lifted up and thou forget the Lord thy God …

But thou shalt remember the Lord thy God for it is He that giveth to thee power to get wealth, that He may establish his covenant which He swore unto thy Fathers as it is this day. And it shall be that if thou at all do forget the Lord thy God and walk after other gods, and serve them, and worship them, I testify against you this day that you will surely perish. As the nations which the Lord destroys before you face, so shall you perish; because you would not be obedient to the voice of the Lord your God. Deuteronomy 8:6-14, 18-20 (KJV).

Clearly, Israel's economic prosperity would be a direct result of their obedience. So important was this concept that Moses had half of the Israelites stand on one hill and half of the Israelites stand on another and recite the exact consequences of obedience and disobedience to each other. The blessings for obedience that they recited are in Deuteronomy 28. There we read:

And it shall come to pass if you shall hearken diligently to the voice of the Lord thy God, to observe and to do all His commandments which I am commanding you this day, that the Lord thy God will set you on high above all nations of the earth. And all these blessings shall come on thee, and overtake you, if you shall hearken unto the voice of the Lord your God. Blessed shall you be in the city and blessed shall you be in the field. Blessed shall be the fruit of your body, and the fruit of your ground, and the fruit of your cattle and the increase of your kine, and the flocks of your sheep. Blessed shall be your basket and your store.

And the Lord shall make you plenteous in goods, and in the fruit of you body, and in the fruit of your cattle, and in the fruit of your ground, in the land which the Lord swore unto your Fathers to give you. The Lord shall open unto you His good treasure, the heavens to give the rain unto your land in his season, and to bless all the works of thine hand: and you shall lend unto many nations and you shall not borrow. And the Lord shall make you the head and not the tail; and you shall be above only, and you shall not be beneath; if you hearken unto the commandments of the Lord thy God, which I command you this day, to observe and to do them. Deuteronomy 28:1-5, 11-13 (KJV).

Economic Prosperity Comes From Obedience

These are economic blessings, and they are directly tied to obedience. When Israel was under the chastening hand of God after they had turned away from Jehovah, Jeremiah (Jeremiah 7:3-7; 22:3-5) promised restoration if they would but turn away from the shedding of innocent blood and the oppression of the stranger, the fatherless, and the widow. In other words, stop abortion, stop inflation (which particularly robs the widows and others on fixed incomes), and stop turning away aliens fleeing oppression in other countries — the strangers that come to our doorstep. What has been the practice of this country for the better part of 2 centuries. Doesn't the Statute of Liberty speak of welcoming the oppressed that come to our shores?[82] There are many other places we could go to as well. When Ezekiel (Ezekiel 34:25-29) speaks of the blessings of the Great Shepherd, he does so in economic terms, saying that the rain would come in its season, and as a result, the produce of the land would yield its fruit in abundance. Even on the return of the Israelites from 70 years of exile, Zechariah (Zechariah 7:9-14) repeats the words of Jeremiah in telling the Israelites that their troubles came as a result of their refusal to obey the Lord. Physical, material, economic, and spiritual blessings flow from cultural obedience to the Word of God. The richest man in the world was the son of the man after God's own heart. Is it any surprise that the unmatched economic prosperity of Israel under Solomon followed one of the most godly kings Israel every had? Our spiritual condition has economic consequences. We cannot expect God's blessing on a nation built on fraud. We cannot expect God's blessing on a nation that so systematically oppresses and impoverishes the poor and the widow[83] with the tax of inflation as this nation does. As a nation that never pays its debts, we can only expect a life of unending servitude.

Disobedience Results in Economic Judgment

If economic blessings are bestowed on obedience, what happens if there is cultural disobedience? You can probably guess without reading more Scripture. Job spells out the plight of the wicked in economic terms in Job 27:16-17 "Though he piles up silver like dust, and prepares garments as plentiful as the day; He may prepare it but the just shall wear it, and the innocent will divide the silver." The future belongs to the people who obey the Word of God. The wealth of the sinner is stored up for the righteous (Pr 13:22), Proverbs tells us, and Solomon adds in Ecclesiastes, "but to the sinner He has given travail, to gather and heap up, that he [i.e., the wicked] may give to the one who is good in God's sight." (Ecclesiastes 2:26) But by far, the most devastating pronouncement of economic curses on disobedience comes in Deuteronomy 28, following the blessings quoted earlier. There Moses told the people:

> But it shall come to pass if you will not hearken unto the voice of the Lord thy God, to observe to do all His commandments and His statutes which I command you this day; that all these curses shall come upon you and overtake you. Deuteronomy 28:15 (KJV)

These curses continue on for over 50 verses. But just to sample some of these warnings, consider:

> "Cursed shall be your basket and your store. Cursed shall be the fruit of your body, and the fruit of your land, the increase of your kine, and the flocks of your sheep. … And you shall grope at noonday as the blind gropes in darkness and you shalt be only oppressed and spoiled evermore and no man shall save you. You shall betroth a wife and another man shall lie with her: you shall build a house and another man shall dwell therein: you shall plant a vineyard and shall not gather the grapes thereof. Your ox will be slain before your eyes and you shall not eat thereof: thine ass shall be violently taken from before your face and shall not be restored to you: your sheep shall be given unto your enemies and you shall have none to rescue them. … The fruit of thy land, and all your labors, shall a nation which you know not eat up; and you shall only be oppressed and crushed alway. The Lord shall bring you and your king which you shall set over you, unto a nation which neither you nor your fathers have known …" Deuteronomy 28:17-18, 29-31, 33, 36 (KJV).

Some of this sounds familiar. Today in this country, people are having their property confiscated through capital forfeiture laws under the guise of fighting the war on drugs. These victims are not felons, drug runners, or money launderers. In many cases, they are simply upright citizens, who for one valid reason or another have some cash. Frequently, the confiscated property is never returned, even though no one is ever convicted or even indicted. Also noteworthy is the loss of national sovereignty that is promised. To be subject to a king other than the one your nation has chosen is to become a slave nation. To be forced to fight and die under the command of foreigners is a huge step toward being subjected to a king you have not chosen. Once again, this is something we are experiencing in America today every time we send our sons (and now our daughters) on UN peacekeeping missions or seek the approval of the United Nations Security Council prior to initiating any military action. Subjecting ourselves to the economic jurisdiction of other nations does nothing to preserve our national freedom. God's curses continue with the following:

You shall carry much seed into the field, and shall gather but little in; for the locust will consume it. You shall plant vineyard and dress them, but shall neither drink of the wine, not gather grapes; for the worms shall eat them. You shall have olive trees throughout all your coasts but you shall not anoint thyself with the oil for your olive will cast his fruit. All the trees and fruit of your land shall the locust consume. He (the stranger that is in your land) shall lend to you and you shall not lend to him: he shall be the head and you shall be the tail. Deuteronomy 28:38-40, 42, 44 (KJV).

These are the mild curses. If you really want to turn your stomach, read the remainder of the chapter. There God speaks of bringing in a fierce nation who would severely oppress Israel and cause a severe famine. Then follows some of the most shocking words in all of scripture.

And thou shalt eat the fruit of thy own body, the flesh of thy sons and daughters, which the Lord thy God hath given thee, in the siege and in the straitness wherewith thine enemies shall distress thee: So that the man that is tender amoung you and very delicate, his eye shall be evil toward his brother, and toward the wife of his bosom, and toward the remnant of his children which he shall leave: So that he will not give to any of them of the flesh of his children whom he shall eat: because he has nothing left him in the siege, and in the straitness, wherewith thine enemy shall distress thee in all thy gates. The tender and delicate woman among you, which would not adventure to set the sole of her foot on upon the ground for delicateness and tenderness, her eye will be evil toward the husband of her bosom and toward her son, and toward her daughter, and toward her young one that cometh out from between her feet, and toward her children which she shall bear: for she shall eat them for want of all things secretly in the siege and straitness wherewith thy enemy shall distress thee in thy gates. Deuteronomy 28:53-57. (KJV)

If you are thinking that this is merely metaphoric language and that such unfathomable cannibalism will not actually occur, consider Ahab's plight in I Kings 17. There, we find a three-year drought that is a result of Ahab's disobedience. [*c.f.* I Kings 18: 18]. Israel persisted in committing abominations and God continued to increase the severity of his judgment on the nation. In II Kings 6, we find an account of a woman eating her own child because of the severity of the famine in the land — exactly as God promised several centuries earlier. Even the wicked king tore his clothes in horror.

But do these curses still apply to us today? Will God still bring us to eat our children if we turn away from obedience to Him? That question is answered for us by Josephus, a Jewish historian who recorded the Roman destruction of Jerusalem by Titus in 70 AD. He recounts the following tale during a siege by Titus:

"Now there was a certain woman that dwelt beyond Jordan, her name was Mary… She was eminent for her family and her wealth and had fled away to Jerusalem with the rest of the multitude and was with them besieged therein at this time. … What she had treasured up, besides [the] food she had contrived to save, had … been carried off by the rapacious guards who came running into her house every day for that purpose. This put the poor woman into a very great passion, … and if she found any food, she perceived her labors were for others, and not for herself; and it was now become impossible for her any way to find any more food; … The famine pierced through her very bowels and marrow, … She then attempted a most unnatural thing; and snatching up her son who was a child sucking at her breast she said,

'O you miserable infant! For whom shall I preserve you in this war, this famine, and this sedition?'... Come on; be you my food, ... As soon as she had said this, she slew her son; and then roasted him, and ate the one half of him and kept the other half by her concealed. Upon this the seditious came in presently and smelling the horrid scent of this food, they threatened her that they would cut her throat immediately if she did show them what food she had gotten ready. She replied that she had saved a very fine portion of it for them; and withal uncovered what was left of her son. ... she said to them, 'This is mine own son and what has been done was mine own doing! ... Come eat of this food for I have eaten of it myself.! Do not you pretend to be more tender than a woman or more compassionate than a mother.'"[84]

The curses in Deuteronomy 28 are curses that God really did and does visit upon peoples and nations who are disobedient to his commandments. The events Josephus describes happened in New Testament times. They certainly can happen again where people fail to obey God's Word. A case might even be made that such judgment is already upon us. Is there really much difference between a mother roasting her child to satisfy her physical hunger and a mother tearing him limb from limb with a knife or vacuum while yet in her womb to satisfy her convenience?

The clear, unavoidable teaching of Scripture is that righteousness exalts a nation, but sin is a reproach to any people. When an economy is built on fraud, theft, and deception, the natural order of things is turned on its ear resulting in broken bodies, broken hearts, broken homes, broken oaths, and broken laws. God will not be mocked. There are cultural consequences for cultural sins. God judges sin. That judgment has economic consequences. No nation, not even America with all its wealth and greatness, can laugh in the face of God, blaspheme his Name, and mock his Word as this nation has done, and expect God to continue to open the storehouse of heaven and provide food in abundance and the rain in its season. But when men devote themselves to glorifying God through developing the earth's productive potential, obeying his laws, and caring for the needy, He will open the windows of heaven for them, causing the earth to yield its fruit in astonishing abundance.[85]

Who Is To Blame?

It is very tempting to blame "the Feds" or "the government" or "the establishment" or even "them" for the economic slavery in which we find ourselves. But these are only symptoms of the problem. The real problem lies in our heart. We have exactly what our parents and grandparents first asked for and what we continue to ask for. In the covetousness of their heart they wanted more money and believed the lie that someone could make it for them with an elastic money supply. This lust of the eyes clouded their understanding and changed our nation from one that required all public officials to take an oath affirming the deity of Jesus Christ[86] and the Old and New Testaments to be the Word of God to a people that don't even know who He is or what he has done. The American people of a previous generation covetously asked for free money, hoping for wealth and riches, and received with it a government that has the ability to steal back our wealth in a way in which not one man in a million can diagnose. The only reason the Federal Reserve Corporation is able to continue this devastating fraud year after year is because we, the American people of this generation, allow it. We want the "good life" that elastic money can buy.

How true are Paul's words to Timothy, "The love of money is the root of all kinds of evil."

Chapter 8

Jehovah Replies

So what's a Christian to do? Stop using greenbacks and live in a cave? Without the right perspective, this story about the federal reserve could be very depressing. How does one begin to unravel the cumulative effect of a century of work to enslave a nation in perpetual debt? Extricating oneself seems so totally hopeless and utterly futile that it is difficult to even think constructively about it. The total inability to escape the effects of the fraud and the seeming utter uselessness of resistance have caused many people to simply ignore the problem. Yes, there have been a few very courageous people who have risked their liberty and family to stand against the fraud. But for the most part, this whole issue is totally ignored by the church. It seems there are bigger fish to fry.

But Scripture has a very different perspective — in fact, it assumes the polar opposite view. Instead of lamenting the seeming futility of resisting large scale conspiracy, Scripture ponders the sanity of anyone who would even think to oppose the reign of Christ. It declares the ultimate futility of conspiring against Messianic rule. We read in Psalm 2:

> Why do the heathen rage, and the people imagine a vain thing? The kings of the earth set themselves, and the rulers take counsel together, against the LORD, and against his anointed, saying, Let us break their bands asunder, and cast away their cords from us.

> He that sits in the heavens shall laugh: the Lord shall have them in derision. Then shall he speak unto them in his wrath, and vex them in his sore displeasure. (Psalm 2:1-5)

Here are people who do not want to acknowledge the lawful authority of the King of Kings, they don't want to be bothered by His laws, and they do not want to live within the institutions He has ordained. To them, marriage is bondage, capital punishment is cruel and unusual, and the gospel is foolishness. This is the rage of the nations. But according to Psalm 2, it is a vain rage. It is a futile, useless, and utterly hopeless effort to plot against the kingship of Jesus Christ.

In our investigation of money and banking, we have came face to face with nothing less than an attack on the Kingship of Jesus Christ. As such, it is doomed to certain failure. The goal of this chapter is to show not only why this is an attack on Christ, but also to outline a biblical response. Ultimately, Scripture provides both great comfort to those who love the Lord Jesus and desire his appearing and a channel of useful activity for the energy that would otherwise feed feelings of futility and despair.

The Universality of the Rage of the Nations

The first thing to realize is that Satan's efforts to incite the kings and people of the earth to overthrow Messiah's reign were not limited to King David's day. The rage of the nations is universal, beginning with Satan's efforts in the Garden of Eden and extending across all of recorded history.

Pharaoh sought to kill off the line of Christ by killing all the male infants in Israel and making slaves of the entire nation.

Athaliah, the wicked daughter of King Ahab, tried to extinguish the line through which the Messiah would be born by killing all the descendants of David.

Herod tried to do the same thing when Christ was born. And a few years later the Jews, the descendants of David himself, fought against the reign of Christ, first putting Christ to death on the cross and then persecuting the Apostles as they preached the gospel of Jesus Christ, announcing that the kingdom of heaven was at hand. We read about an example of this in Acts 4.

When the Apostles faced opposition to their preaching, they recognized it as an attack on Christ himself. They realized that this was exactly what David had spoken of in Psalm 2. In verse 24 of Acts 4, we read that when the Apostles related to the church what had happened before the Sanhedrin, they were reminded of Psalm 2. They connected the opposition of the rulers of the Jews to their preaching with what God had said in Psalm 2 by the mouth of his servant David:

> And when they heard that, they lifted up their voice to God with one accord, and said, Lord, thou art God, which hast made heaven, and earth, and the sea, and all that in them is: Who by the mouth of thy servant David hast said, Why did the heathen rage, and the people imagine vain things? The kings of the earth stood up, and the rulers were gathered together against the Lord, and against his Christ. For of a truth against thy holy child Jesus, whom thou hast anointed, both Herod, and Pontius Pilate, with the Gentiles, and the people of Israel, were gathered together, For to do whatsoever thy hand and thy counsel determined before to be done. And now, Lord, behold their threatenings: and grant unto thy servants, that with all boldness they may speak thy word, … (Act 4:24-29)

In seeking to stop the Apostles from preaching the gospel, the Sanhedrin was attacking Christ himself, they were challenging the Kingship of Jesus Christ. They were saying in effect, "Who made you to be a king over us? Why should we have to listen to Your messengers?"

Recognizing the Attack Today

This attack against the reign of Christ did not end with the Apostles of the New Testament church. It continues today. In its simplest form, the rage of the nations against the rule of Christ is an attempt to squash the preaching of the gospel and the practice of the Christian faith. We have this today in many parts of the world. But Satan is far more clever and crafty than to limit his warfare to these simple means. For often, such outright persecution causes the church to grow. His attack today in our country is far more subtle. But despite its many forms, the raging of the kings and nations spoken of in this Psalm can always be recognized by the fact that it seeks to challenge at its root the authority through which Christ rules.

Christ rules through three institutions: the family, the church, and the state, or the civil government. The King is God's servant, (magistrate comes from the Latin meaning greater servant) ordained by God to reward those that do well and to carry out God's vengeance on those that do evil. The pastor is God's minister (that is Latin for lesser servant) ordained to teach and to shepherd God's people. The great commission given to the church is to make disciples of all nations, baptizing them into the Father, Son, and Holy Spirit and teaching them all that the Lord has commanded. Parents are also God's servants, commanded to teach the next generation the fear of the Lord. Each of these three areas (i.e., family, church, and state) are strategic strongholds and subject to Satan's most desperate attacks.

If Satan can eviscerate the authority of parents to train their children to fear the Lord and command their children after them, then he will destroy families as surely as Pharaoh's murder of the male infants of Israel.

If Satan can induce the nations of the earth to blunt and pervert the civil magistrate so that those who do well are punished and those that do evil are rewarded, he will have succeeded in leading many people into sin as effectively as King Ahab led Israel into idolatry.

If Satan can bring the church to doubt just some of God's Word, or fail to preach the Scriptures in their entirety and apply them to every area of life, the pure milk of the word will be corrupted as surely as the Pharisees perverted Scripture and thereby kept many out of the kingdom of heaven.

Indeed, this is exactly what we do see when we look all around us. The church in our country today is prohibited from applying Scripture to every area of life. It is told you can preach all you want about Christ, just don't apply his Word to the civil magistrate.[87] When churches attain tax exempt status as a 501(c)3 corporation, they are saying in effect that, as an institution, they are subordinate to the civil magistrate and subject to taxation. In accepting tax exempt status, they are accepting a government subsidy, and, as with all government subsidies, there are strings attached. One such string is that the church will not apply the precepts of Scripture to political candidates or issues. Consequently, when was the last time you heard a sermon that applied God's Word to issues such as the criteria for a just war, the injustice and greed associated with the progressive income tax, or the unbiblical proposals of political candidates. One church, Pierce Creek Church in Binghamton, NY did raise moral questions about William Clinton's candidacy through ads placed in national periodicals just prior to the 1992 elections. Even though the ads stopped short of recommending that Mr. Clinton not be elected, the church promptly lost its tax-exempt status retroactive for the whole year. They had not recommended how people ought to vote.[88] They simply raised some questions. Clearly, Pierce Creek Presbyterian Church lost its tax exempt status for applying the scriptural qualifications for civil rulers to the presidential candidates. *How many other churches failed to say anything?*

The attack on the family is probably even more fierce. As Psalm 78 and Romans 3:2 make so clear, it is this passing on from parents to children the wonderful works of the Lord that is the blessing and advantage of the covenant child. Proverbs commands parents to train up a child in the way he should go.[89] This does not mean we ask our children in which direction they want to go. It means we set before them the way they should go and command them to walk therein. In training a tree, a farmer does not find the natural bent of the tree and stake it accordingly; rather, he drives the stake in the ground according to the way the tree ought to grow and then bends the tree to conform to the stake. This is the biblical model for training our children.[90] This ability and authority of Christian parents to teach their children the fear and admonition of the Lord is the primary means that God has ordained for the extension of his church. Whoever seeks to destroy the authority of parents to biblically train their children is attempting, like Herod of old, to destroy the church, which is nothing less than conspiring to overthrow Messiah's reign.

For example, we find the authority God has given to parents to train up their children in the fear and admonition of the Lord being directly attacked and supplanted by the United Nations in treaties such as the *UN Convention on the Rights of the Child.* This document attempts to remove parents from their God-given role of caretaker, provider, tutor, and trainer of their children, and gives to children the ability to execute their own will in nearly all matters. Such a notion cuts at the very root of the commands in Deuteronomy 6 and elsewhere[91] to set before our children the way of the Lord and command them to walk in it after us. The Lord praised Abraham for his obedience in this regard[92] and as a result brought upon him the blessing he had promised. A document like the *UN Convention on the Rights of the Child* makes it illegal for parents to do what the Lord requires of them. It is an attempt to prevent parents from passing on to their children the Christian faith. Running coaches tell us that relay races are often won or lost in the passing of the baton. So it is with the faith. When it is lost, it is usually in the passing from one generation to the next.

Government schooling is another example. While Christians are sometimes confused about the ultimate goal of such schools, the enemies of Christ don't seem to be. Consider the following excerpt discovered in the minutes of the Carnegie Endowment for International Peace by Norman Dodd, director of research for the House Committee to Investigate Tax Exempt Foundations in the 1950's.

> [In the minutes] the trustees raised a question. And they discussed the question and the question was specific, "Is there any means known to man more effective than war, assuming you wish to alter the life of an entire people?" And they discussed this and at the end of a year they came to the conclusion that there was no more effective means to that end known to man. So, then they raised question number two and the question was, "How do we involve the United States in a war?" ...Finally, we were in a war. These trustees, in a meeting about 1917 had the brashness to congratulate themselves on the wisdom of their original decision because already the impact of the war had indicated it would alter life and can alter life in this country. ... The war was over. Then the concern became, as expressed by the trustees, seeing to it that there was no reversion to life in this country as it existed prior to 1914. And they came to the conclusion that to prevent a reversion they must control education. And then they approached the Rockefeller Foundation and they said, "Will you take on the acquisition of the control of education as it involves subjects that are domestic in their significance? We'll take it on the basis of subjects that have an international significance." And it was agreed. Then, together, they decided that the key to it is the teaching of American history and they must change that.[93]

These men understood the great importance of education. They knew that education is the way to change a society.[94] They knew that to rule the world they had to have control of education. It really does matter who writes the history textbooks. According to Jeroboam's version of history, some golden calves delivered the children of Israel from Egypt. According to Moses' version, Jehovah delivered the children of Israel from the house of bondage. In teaching his version, Jeroboam brought God's judgment on his land. That's why government education would like our children at younger and younger ages — to get Jeroboam's version of history to our children before their parents can teach them Moses' version.

In May 1949, the Bureau of Educational Research for Ohio State University published a test for children in grades 4 to 7 entitled *The Wishing Well*. It contained statements in the form of wishes. The students were to check the ones that applied to them. Some examples were:

1) I wish I did not feel so different from my parents.

2) I wish I knew how you can believe that God is always right and at the same time believe that you should think for yourself.

A few months earlier the United Nations Educational, Scientific & Cultural Organization, often referred to by its initials UNESCO, published a series of booklets titled, *Towards World Understanding* in which we read in Volume 5, "Kindergarten has a significant part to play in the child's education … not only can it correct many of the errors of home training, it can prepare the child for membership in the world society."

A year earlier, in 1948, the director of the World Health Organization published an article in which he said that, "We have swallowed all manner of poisonous certainties fed us by our parents, our Sunday School teachers and priests." He went on to say that one of the objectives of the new education was the eradication of the concept of right and wrong as the basis for training children.[95]

Today, Christian parents often battle the disciples of these ideas — people whose goal is to remove children from the hands of "harmful" parents who teach their children in the fear and admonition of the Lord.

This is nothing less than a direct attack on Christ and his Kingship. This is the work of people who are crying, "Let us break his bonds in pieces, let us cast his cords away." It is terrifying to contemplate. But consider the reply of Almighty God to the rage of the nations.

God's Reply To The Rage Of The Nations

He who sits in the heavens shall laugh. The Lord shall hold them in derision. Then he shall speak to them in his wrath and terrify them in his deep displeasure.

The outcome is certain. All the nations in the world are but as a speck of dust on the scales compared to the power of our Creator King. This is our King, this is our Defender. He has created heaven and earth. He has created these men. Each breath they take, each beat of their heart, each second of their life is God's gift to them. It is Yahweh that has raised up these nations and peoples, it is with his permission and authority that they rule.

He is not intimidated by the armies of the earth arrayed against him. In fact, he holds them in derision.[96] To the King who dwells in the heavens in unapproachable light, the greatest efforts of the kings of the earth are like the tantrums of a little infant.

When the power of man appears overwhelming to us and God's deliverance seems to tarry, it is a great comfort to remember that it is simply God's time for laughter and quiet contempt.

But this is just the beginning of God's reply to the raging of the nations. When he is done laughing, then he will speak to them in his wrath. The weapons of his warfare are not swords and guns, but the power of his Word. Those who dare to oppose the Kingship of Jesus Christ, who reject his authority, who want to cast his law aside, who want to stop parents from teaching their children the fear of the Lord, who want to stop the civil magistrate from bringing God's vengeance on those that do evil, and who want to shut the mouth of the church from proclaiming the gospel, will be broken in God's wrath as easily and completely as a sledgehammer smashing china dolls.

God's decree is "I have installed my King upon my holy hill." To this King, he says, "You are my Son, today I have begotten you.

Ask of Me and I will give you the nations for your inheritance." God is saying, I have already anointed the one to rule the world and it is my Son, not the kings of earth who take counsel together against him. God tells the wicked his will has already been written and they are not in it. The kingdoms of the world belong to him and he has given them to his only Begotten Son. He is the sole heir of all things. God is declaring for all the world to hear the deity, the glory, the power, and the dominion of his Son over all the kingdoms of this earth.[97]

In Revelation, we read that the testimony of the those around the throne in heaven is that the kingdoms of this world have become the kingdoms of our Lord and of his Christ, his Anointed One. All who do not submit themselves to the sovereignty of Christ as the King above all other Kings make war against God and His Anointed. Those who make war against the Son, do so to their eternal peril. God holds them in derision, laughs at the futility of their puny effort, and then destroys them when his anger is kindled just a little.

Pharaoh thought he was fighting a nation of poor Hebrew slaves. "Who is Jehovah," he mocked? God answered him in his wrath and left him without an army or an heir.

Goliath thought he was taunting a nation of cowards whose carcasses he could give the birds. But in fact, he was taunting the living God himself. God answered those taunts in his wrath and the birds ate his flesh.

Herod, Pontius Pilate, and the Jews thought they were fighting a carpenter from Nazareth and some untrained fishermen. Having crucified Jesus, they thought they had won a great victory. The book of Revelation is a solemn and terrifying testament to the awful judgments God poured on those that crucified the Lord of Glory.

But these displays of God's power pale in comparison to the power displayed in Christ's death and resurrection. This act of God's power far outshines every other display of God's power throughout history. Yes, God is glorified in the judgment of the wicked. Yes, those who seek to overthrow the rule of Christ today by preventing parents from exercising their authority, by stopping the proclamation of the gospel, or by perverting the punishment of evildoers will see the glory of God displayed in terrible judgment. But God's glory is even more brilliantly displayed in the conversion of the wicked — in subduing to himself those that once fought against him. That is why the glory of the kingdom of heaven was not fully manifest until God raised Jesus Christ from the dead. The risen Christ, the King of Kings, now goes out conquering by the power of his word — the sword of his Spirit.

This is what Yaweh means in saying to his Son, "Ask of Me and I will give you the nations for your inheritance, the ends of the earth for your possession." The kingdoms of the earth have always belonged to the Lord. But with the coming of the kingdom of heaven, God now brings the power of his Word, the gospel, to all nations. He has always been the Sovereign Ruler of Heaven and Earth, casting down nations and kings that rebelled against him and raising others up. But now, in the person of his Son, he is conquering all nations with his Word. Where before only one nation knew his Word, now all the nations of the earth will be conquered by the gospel. Those that once rebelled against him now willingly bend their knees before him. Those that once fought against his law, now take his yoke upon them and learn of him. The reply of the King of Kings to the raging of the nations against his kingdom is to conquer all his enemies. Some are conquered in his grace and others are conquered in his wrath. But all are conquered.

This Psalm unites grace and judgment in the Kingship of Jesus Christ. Both are aspects of his reign. He is crowned in glory both in his work of judgment and in his work of grace.

The response of wisdom to the coronation of Christ is to submit willingly to the King of Kings, to be conquered by his grace and not conquered by his wrath, to stop plotting how to escape his authority and overthrow his rule in our life, and to begin serving him in fear and rejoicing in his grace with trembling. The response of wisdom is to pay homage to him – to kiss the Son.

The kiss is an image from the royal court. It is the sign of honor that subjects gave to a sovereign. Kings would extend their hand to those that approached their throne. When people kissed the royal hand extended to them, they were both acknowledging the sovereignty of the one being kissed, and affirming their readiness to fight in battle for him. How does this apply to us today? How do we fight for him?

The Apostle Peter thought that meant he needed to swing a sword of steel to cut off the ear of those that were fighting against his Lord.

But Christ rebuked him for that attempt at service in the Garden of Gethsemane, and by the time he is arrested by the Jews in Acts 4, there is a very different response.

Recognizing that the opposition they faced from the leaders of the Jews was the opposition to the rule of Christ spoken of in Psalm 2, the Apostles pray for boldness to proclaim God's Word.[98] Clearly, those who would kiss the Son and fight as good soldiers of Jesus Christ are to do so with the Word of God. Our sword in this war is the Word of God; our shield is faith in Jesus Christ.

This spiritual war is waged on three primary fronts: by the church, by the family, and by the civil government. It is waged as pastors teach the people to observe everything God has commanded; as parents train their children in the fear and admonition of the Lord; and as kings rule according to the word of God.

This means the church must believe and teach all of Scripture, from Genesis to Revelation, but especially the Scripture that is being attacked. For example, today the Genesis account of creation is being attacked. If the church is to engage in the battle as good soldiers of Jesus Christ, it must unashamedly believe and clearly proclaim the creation account of Genesis 1, wherein in 6 days God made the world and all that is in it. It must defend, without embarrassment, the Scripture's clear teaching on the age of the earth and not silently accept scientific claims that God's creation is millions or billions of years old. The authority and credibility of God's Word is at stake. Anything less is to fail to carry out her great commission and compromise with unbelief.[99]

For parents, this means that they must teach their children the truth about the world God made in the light of the Word God gave. The Lord will use our children to extend his kingdom long after we have ceased our earthly warfare. This idea is expressed in Psalm 127 which speaks about children as the heritage of the Lord saying, "...the fruit of the womb is his reward, as arrows are in the hand of a mighty man; so are the children of ones youth."[100] They are the weapons of godly men which the Lord uses to combat those who are seeking to overthrow his reign.

What's a Christian to Do?

This brings us back to the question which opened this chapter, "What is a Christian to do?" Like polygamy, there is no simple solution for the current generation. This problem was not created in a day, and it won't be solved in a day. But there are two things people ought to do that will have a huge impact. First, get your children (or grandchildren) out of government schools. Why give your arrows to those who are fighting against the Lord?

I realize that there are Christian teachers and administrators in government schools and Christian board members overseeing government schools. However, as an institution, government schools in all fifty states usurp the authority of parents, claiming that the responsibility to educate children belongs to them. They give children a false god by failing to teach as truth that they were created by God and will one day answer to him for everything they have done.[101] They require students to tolerate false religions (e.g., Humanism) by forbidding the public acknowledgement of God and the proclamation of His Word on government property.[102]

Secondly, and equally important, faithfully and formally teach your children — and grandchildren — the word of God.

This ministry of the Word to their children is one of the chief callings of every Christian parent. Paul told Timothy that from a child he had known the Scriptures which were able to make him wise unto salvation having been instructed in them by his mother and grandmother. Paul expressed confidence that the faith which first dwelt in his mother and grandmother now dwelt in Timothy. This is the usual and ordinary means by which God establishes his covenant and builds his church. God has promised to be a God to us and to our children. He declares our children to be holy, to be set apart from the world.[103] But they are born in sin. Like everyone else that has ever been saved, they too must cry out to God for his saving grace.

How shall they call on Him in whom they have not believed? How shall they believe in Him whom they have not heard? And how shall they hear without a preacher? Faith comes by hearing and hearing by the word of God. Paul tells us in Romans 3:2 that to have the oracles of God — to live each day under the ministry of parents who take as much care in feeding their children the Word as they do in providing them bread and clothes — is the benefit of a covenant child.

There are many aspects to this service or ministry. Family worship is the first that comes to mind. It certainly is one of the most important. In fact, family worship was considered such an important aspect of the ministry of the word by fathers and mothers in their homes that when the Westminster Standards were drafted in the 1640s, they wrote not only the well known creeds and directory for public worship, but also a directory for family worship.

Our homes are to be a model of the church. Whether or not you have children at home or even if you do not have any children yet, the reading of scripture, prayer, and singing should be a daily habit. Keep a Bible near the dinner table and don't get up from a meal without also opening the Word of Life. What better illustration is there of the fact that man does not live by bread alone but by every word that proceeds from the mouth of God. We must daily exhort our households to obedience and encourage them with the tender love of a shepherd to follow Christ. If family worship is a new concept to you, start by simply reading the Bible and asking simple Who, What, Where, When, and How questions of the text. If that is too much of a challenge, simply read the Bible without comment. It doesn't have to be long; it just has to be regular.

Another aspect of this ministry is the memorization of Scripture. Most parents have a formal program—whether they do it themselves or hire someone else to do it—for teaching their children math facts. Things like 8 x 8 = 64. Many consider these facts important enough to memorize. What about the Word of God? Do you have a program in your home to memorize the Bible? Not just John 3:16 and 1 John 1:9, but whole chapters and books of the Bible? When a young man or woman leaves your home, how much of the Bible is hid in their heart? When our children leave our homes they may forget our prayers, they may forget our words of advice; they may even throw away their godly habits and the Bible we bought them for graduation. But they will not be able to throw away the words of Scripture impressed into their memory. This is an important means of grace for all of God's people, but particularly children.

Hand in hand with the memorization of Scripture is the memorization of the catechism. This form of sound words systematizes the teaching of

Scripture. Learning the catechism enables one to better understand how Scripture is related to itself, how it fits together as a unified coherent system of truth. If provides a framework to begin to put together different passages of Scripture with common themes. The catechism speaks to our intellectual dimension.

Because we are ignorant, we need Christ to declare to us by his Word and Spirit the will of God for our salvation. Our children are also born ignorant. In a lesser but analogous way we as parents must declare to our children the word of God; we must, as Psalm 78 commands, tell them of God's wonderful works in history.

> Give ear, O my people, to my law: incline your ears to the words of my mouth. I will open my mouth in a parable: I will utter dark sayings of old: Which we have heard and known, and our fathers have told us. We will not hide them from their children, showing to the generation to come the praises of the LORD, and his strength, and his wonderful works that he hath done. For he established a testimony in Jacob, and appointed a law in Israel, which he commanded our fathers, that they should make them known to their children: That the generation to come might know them, even the children which should be born; who should arise and declare them to their children: That they might set their hope in God, and not forget the works of God, but keep his commandments: And might not be as their fathers, a stubborn and rebellious generation; a generation that set not their heart aright, and whose spirit was not steadfast with God. The children of Ephraim, being armed, and carrying bows, turned back in the day of battle. They kept not the covenant of God, and refused to walk in his law; And forgot his works, and his wonders that he had showed them. Psa 78:1-11 (KJV)

Yes, it is true that our children may not understand all that they are memorizing. But that is O.K. Later, when they are older and do understand they will have a treasure of wisdom already within them. There is nothing that can take it away. Even at the height of the communist persecution, they never learned to take away what Christians had hidden in their heart.

In addition to family worship, Scripture memory, and catechizing, the ministry of the Scriptures to our children must also include prayer.

We must pray with them and for them. Job regularly prayed for his children that God would be merciful to them and forgive them if they had sinned. Like a priest, he interceded for them before the throne of grace. So must we.

Instructing our children in the Word of God does not consist simply in communication of knowledge and exhortation and encouragement to obedience. It must also include correction when they disobey the Word of God. This is not punishment. The civil magistrate is charged with executing the wrath of God on those that do evil. The discipline that is a part of the ministry of the Word by parents to their children is done in love and compassion. It is like the chastisement God sends to his children. It's purpose is not to punish, but to train.

Parents also minister the word to their covenant children by their example. In fact, it would not be an exaggeration to say that if a picture is worth a thousand words, our example is worth a thousand pictures. Paul told Timothy, one of the earliest pastors in the New Testament church, "be an example to the believers, in word, in conduct, in love, in spirit, in faith, in purity." His example was an important part of his preaching ministry of the Word. In the same way, an important part of the ministry of the word by parents to their children is their example. This is the significance of the well–known command in Deuteronomy 6 to teach our children as we rise up, lie down, and walk by the way. A child's first sensation of love is from his mother's hand, the first words he hears come from his mother's mouth. What sort of words are they? By the time your child is 2 or 3 years old and you want to teach him to sing praises to his heavenly Father, to say this is the day the Lord has made, we will rejoice and be glad in it, he has already learned from your example exactly what you think of each day the Lord has given. If what you try to teach him does not match what you have already taught him, you'll never get very far.

These are most encouraging words for fathers and mothers who are daily discipling their little ones. The hours parents spend each day in raising a godly family, in teaching them the word of God by precept and example, are hours spent serving the Lord. The ministry of the Word by parents to their children are the arrows which God uses to defeat the kings and peoples fighting against him and advance his kingdom throughout the earth. A nation of such people will not tolerate the dollar non¢ents of the Federal Reserve Corporation nor the civil magistrates who do.

Appendix I

Mechanics of Fractional Reserve Banking

Thus through stage after stage of expansion, money can grow to a total of 10 times the new reserves supplied to the banking system ...

as the new deposits created by loans at each stage are added to those created at all earlier stages and those supplied by the initial reserve-creating action.[104]

Initial Deposit $10,000

Assets				**Liabilities**
Expansion Stage	**Reserves**	**Excess**	**Loans**	**Deposits**
Deposit	1,000	9,000	--	10,000
1	1,900	8,100	9,000	19,000
2	2,710	7,290	17,100	27,100
3	3,439	6,561	24,390	34,390
4	4,095	5,905	30,951	40,951
5	4,686	5,314	36,856	46,856
6	5,217	4,783	42,170	52,170

7	5,695	4,305	46,953	56,953
8	6,126	3,874	51,258	61,258
9	6,513	3,487	55,132	65,132
10	6,862	3,138	58,619	68,619
20	8,906	1,094	79,058	89,058
Final	10,000	0	90,000	100,000

Figure 9. The Mechanics of Fractional Reserve Banking

This chart assumes a reserve requirement of 10%. The first deposit of $10,000 results in a required reserve of $1,000 and $9,000 in *excess* reserves that can be loaned. When these $9,000 are loaned out, they become deposits in some other bank account. There are now $19,000 available for deposit in the economy at large. From the additional $9,000 of deposits, there is created an additional $900 reserve requirement leaving an excess of $8100 which can be loaned out. This process continues as the money ripples throughout the economy. The net effect is to increase the funds available for deposit from $10,000 to a theoretical limit of $100,000.

Appendix 2

Congressional Record –House December 22, 1913

[Page 1430]

MR. GLASS. Mr. Speaker, I present the conference report (H. Rept. 163) on the bill H. R. 7837, the currency bill, and, under the order of the House I ask for its immediate consideration.

[Omitted]

The Speaker. … The Clerk will read the report.

The Clerk read as follows

Conference Report (H. Rept. No. 163)

The committee of conference on the disagreeing votes of the two Houses on the amendment of the Senate to the bill (H. R. 7837) to provide for the establishment of Federal reserve banks, ***to furnish an elastic currency***, [emphasis added] to afford means of rediscounting commercial paper, to establish a more effective supervision of banking in the United States, and for other purposes, having met, after full and free conference have agreed to recommend and do recommend to their respective Houses as follows:

> That the House recede from its disagreement to the amendment of the Senate and agree to the same with an amendment as follows:

In lieu of the amendment proposed by the Senate insert the following:

Be it enacted, etc., That the Short title of this act shall be the "Federal reserve act."

Wherever the word "bank" is used in this act, the word shall be held to include State bank, banking association and trust company, except where national backs or Federal reserve banks are specifically referred to.

The terms "national bank" and "national banking association" used in this act shall be held to be synonymous and interchangeable. The term "member bank" shall be held to mean any national bank State bank, or bank or trust company which has become a member of one of the reserve banks created by this act. The term "board" shall be held to mean Federal reserve board; the term "district" shall be held to mean Federal reserve district; the term "reserve bank" shall be held to mean Federal reserve bank.

Federal Reserve Districts

Sec. 2. As soon as practicable the Secretary of the Treasury, the Secretary of Agriculture and the Comptroller of the Currency, acting as "the reserve bank organization committee," shall designate not less than 8 nor more than 12 cities to be known as Federal reserve cities, and shall divide the continental United States, excluding Alaska, into districts, each district to contain only one of such Federal reserve cities. The determination of said organization committee shall not be subject to review except by the Federal reserve board when organized: Provided, That the districts shall be apportioned with due regard to the convenience and customary course of business and shall not necessarily be coterminous with any State or States. The districts thus created may be readjusted and new districts may from time to time be created by the Federal reserve board, not to exceed 12 in all. Such districts shall be known as Federal reserve districts and may be designated by number. A majority of the organization committee shall constitute a quorum with authority to act.

Said organization committee shall be authorized to employ counsel and expert aid, to take testimony, to send for persons and papers, to administer oaths, and to make such investigation as may be deemed necessary by the said committee in determining the reserve districts and in designating the cities within such districts where such Federal reserve banks Shall be severally located. The said committee shall supervise the organization in each of the cities designated of a Federal reserve bank which shall include in its title the name of the city in which it is situated, as "Federal Reserve Bank of Chicago."

Under regulations to be prescribed by the organization committee, every national banking association in the United States is hereby required, and every eligible bank in the United States and every trust company within the District of Columbia is hereby authorized to signify in writing, within 60 days after the Massage of this act, its acceptance of the terms aunt provisions hereof. When the organization committee shall have designated the cities in which Federal reserve banks are to be organized, and fixed the geographical limits of the Federal reserve districts, every national banking association within that district shall be required within 30 days after notice from the [Page 1431] organization committee, to subscribe to the capital stock of such Federal reserve bank in a sum equal to 6 per cent of the paid-up capital stock and surplus of such bank, one-sixth of the subscription to be payable on call of the organization committee or of the Federal reserve board, one-sixth within three months and one-sixth within six months thereafter, and the remainder of the subscription or any part thereof shall be subject to rill when deemed necessary by the Federal reserve board, said payments to be in gold or gold certificates.

The shareholders of every Federal reserve bank shall be held individually responsible, equally and ratably, and not one for another, for all contracts, debts, and engagements of such bank to the extent of the amount of their subscriptions to such stock at the par value thereof in addition to the amount subscribed, whether such subscriptions have been paid up in whole or in part under the provisions of this act.

Any national bank failing to signify its acceptance of the terms of this act within the 60 days aforesaid, shall cease to act as a reserve agent, upon 30 days' notice, to be given within the discretion of the said organization committee or of the Federal reserve board.

Should any national banking association in the United States now organized fail within one year after the passage of this act to become a member bank or fail to comply with any of the provisions of this act applicable thereto, all of the rights, privileges, and franchises of such association granted to it under the national-bank act, or under the provisions of this act shall be thereby forfeited. Any noncompliance with or violation of this act shall, however, be determined and adjudged by any court of the United States of competent jurisdiction in a suit brought for that purpose in the district or territory in which such bank is located, under direction of the Federal reserve board, by the Comptroller of the Currency in his own name Defuse the association shall be declared dissolved. In cases of such noncompliance or violation, other than the failure to become a member bank under the provisions of this act every director who participated in or assented to the same shall be held liable in his person, or individual capacity for all damages said bank, its shareholders, or any other person shall sustained in consequence of such violation.

Such dissolution shall not take away or impair any remedy against such corporation, its stockholders or officers, for any liability or penalty which shall been previously incurred.

Should the subscriptions by banks to the stock of said Federal reserve bank or any one or more of them be, in the judgment of the organization committee, insufficient to provide the amount of capital required therefor, then and in that event the said organization committee may, under conditions and regulations to be prescribed by it, offer to public subscription at par such an amount of stock in said Federal reserve banks, or any one or more of them, as said committee shall determine, subject to the same conditions as to payment and stock liability as provided for member banks.

No individual, copartnership, or corporation other than a member bank of its district shall be permitted to subscribe for or to hold at any time more than $25,000 par value of stock in any Federal reserve bank.

Such stock shall be known as public stock and may be transferred on the books of the Federal reserve bank by the chairman of the board of directors of such bank.

Should the total subscriptions by banks and the public to the stock of said Federal reserve banks or any one or more of them, be, in the judgment of the organization committee insufficient to provide the amount of capital required therefor, then and in that event the said organization committee shall allot to the United States such an amount of said stock as said committee shall determine. Said United States stock shall be paid for at par out of any money in the Treasury not otherwise appropriated and shall be held by the Secretary of the Treasury and disposed of for the benefit of the United States in such manner, at such times and at such price, not less than par, as the Secretary of the Treasury shall determine.

Stock not held by member banks shall not be entitled to voting power.

The Federal reserve board is hereby empowered to adopt and promulgate roles and regulations governing the transfers of said stock.

No Federal reserve bank shall commence business with a subscribed capital less than $4,000,000. The organization of reserve districts and Federal reserve cities shall not be construed as changing the present status of reserve cities and central reserve cities, except in so far as this act changes the amount of reserves that may be carried with approved reserve agents located therein. The organization committee shall have power to appoint such assistants and incur such expenses in carrying out the provisions of this act as it shall deem necessary, and such expenses shall be payable by the Treasurer of the United States upon voucher approved by the Secretary of the Treasury, and the sum of $100,000 or so much thereof as may be necessary is hereby appropriated, out of any moneys in the Treasury not otherwise appropriated for the payment of such expenses.

Branch Offices

Sec. 3. Mach Federal reserve bank shall establish branch banks within the Federal reserve district in which it is located and may do so in the district of any Federal reserve bank which may have been suspended. Such branches shall be operated by a board of directors under rules and regulations approved by the Federal reserve board. Directors of branch banks shall possess the same qualifications as directors of the Federal reserve banks. Four of said directors shall be selected by the reserve bank and three by the Federal reserve board, and they shall hold office during the pleasure, respectively, of the parent bank and the Federal reserve board. The reserve bank shall designate one of the directors as manager.

Federal Reserve Banks

Sec. 4. When the organization committee shall have established Federal reserve districts as provided in section 2 of this act, a certificate shall be filed with the Comptroller of the Currency showing the geographical limits of such districts and the Federal reserve city designated in each of such districts. The Comptroller of the Currency shall thereupon cause to be forwarded to each national bank located in each district, and to such outer banks declared to be eligible by the organization committee which may apply therefor, an application blank in form to be approved by the organization committee, which blank shall contain a resolution to be adopted by the board of directors of each bank executing such application authorizing a subscription to the capital stock of the Federal reserve bank organizing in that district in accordance with the provisions of this act.

When the minimum amount of capital stock prescribed by this act for the organization of any Federal reserve bank shall have been subscribed and allotted, the organization committee shall designate any five banks of those whose applications have been received, to execute a certificate of organization, and thereupon the banks so designated shall, under their seals, make an organization certificate which shall specifically state the name of such Federal reserve bank, the territorial extent of the district over which the operations of such Federal reserve bank are to be carried on the city and State in which said bank is to be located, the amount of capital stock and the number of shares into which the same is divided, the name and place of doing business of each bank executing such certificate, and of all banks which have subscribed to the capital stock of such Federal reserve bank and the number of shares subscribed by each, and the fact that the certificate is made to enable those banks executing same, and of all banks which have subscribed or may thereafter subscribe to the capital stock of such Federal reserve bank to avail themselves of the advantages of this act.

The said organization certificate shall be acknowledged before a judge of some court of record or notary public; and shall be, together with the acknowledgement thereof, authenticated by the seal of such court, or notary, transmitted to the Comptroller of the Currency, who shall file, record and carefully preserve the same in his office.

Upon the filing of such certificate with the Comptroller of the Currency as aforesaid, the said Federal reserve bank shall become a body corporate and as such, and in the name designated in such organization certificate, shall have power:

First. ***To adopt and use a corporate seal.*** [Emphasis added.]

Second. To have succession for a period of 20 years from its organization unless it is sooner dissolved by an act of Congress or unless its franchise becomes forfeited by some violation of law.

Third. To make contracts.

Fourth. ***To sue and be sued, complain and defend in any court of law or equity.***

Fifth. To appoint by its board of directors, such officers and employees as are not otherwise provided for in this act, to define their duties, require bonds of them and fix the penalty thereof, and to dismiss at pleasure such officers or employees.

Sixth. To prescribe by its board of directors by-laws, not inconsistent with law, regulating the manner in which its general business may be conducted, and the privileges granted to it by law may be exercised and enjoyed.

Seventh. To exercise by its board of directors or duly authorized officers or agents, all powers specifically granted by the provisions of this act and such incidental powers as shall be necessary to carry on the business of banking within the limitations prescribed by this act. [Page 1432]

Eighth. Upon deposit with the Treasurer of the United States of any bonds of the United States in the manner provided by existing law

> relating to national banks, to receive from the comptroller of the Currency circulating notes in blank registered and countersigned as provided by law equal in amount to the par value of the bonds so deposited, such note to be issued under the same conditions and provisions of law as relate to the issue of circulating notes of national banks secured by bonds of the United States bearing the circulating privilege, except that the issue of such notes shall not be flushed to the capital stock of such Federal reserve bank.

But no Federal reserve bank shall transact any business except such as is incidental and necessarily preliminary to its organization until it has been authorized by the Comptroller of the Currency to commence business under the provisions of this act.

Every Federal reserve bank shall be conducted under the supervision and control of a board of directors.

The board of directors shall perform the duties usually appertaining to the office of directors of banking associations and all such duties as are prescribed by law.

Said board shall administer the affairs of said bank fairly and impartially and without discrimination in favor of or against any member bank or banks and shall, subject to the provisions of law and the orders of the Federal reserve board, extend to each member bank such discounts, advancements and accommodations as may be safely and reasonably made with due regard for the claims and demands of other member banks.

Such board of directors shall be selected as hereinafter specified and shall consist of nine members, holding office for three years, and divided into three classes, designated as classes A, B, and C.

Class A shall consist of three members, who shall be chosen by and be representative of the stockholding banks.

Class B shall consist of three members, who at the time of their election shall be actively engaged in their district in commerce, agriculture, or some other industrial pursuit.

Class C shall consist of three members who shall be designated by the Federal reserve board. When the necessary subscriptions to the capital stock have been obtained for the organization of any Federal reserve bank, the Federal reserve board shall appoint the class C directors and shall designate one of such directors as chairman of the board to be selected. Pending the designation of such chairman, the organization committee shall exercise the powers and duties appertaining to the office of chairman in the organization of such Federal reserve bank.

No Senator or Representative in Congress shall be a member of the Federal reserve board or an officer or a director of a Federal reserve bank.

No director of class B shall be an officer, director, or employee of any bank.

No director of class C shall be an officer, director, employee, or stockholder of any bank.

Directors of class A and class B shall be chosen in the following manner:

The chairman of the board of directors of the Federal reserve bank of the district in which the bank is situated or, pending the appointment of such chairman, the organization committee shall classify the member banks of the district into three general groups or divisions. Each group shall contain as nearly as may be third of the aggregate number of the member banks of the district and shall consist, as nearly as may be, of banks of similar capitalization. The groups shall be designated by number by the chairman.

At a regularly called meeting of the board of directors of each member bank in the district it shall elect by ballot a district reserve elector and shall certify his name to the chairman of the board of directors of the Federal reserve bank of the district. The chairman shall make lists of the district reserve electors thus named by banks in each of the aforesaid three groups and shall transmit one list to each elector in each group.

Each member bank shall be permitted to nominate to the chairman one candidate for director of class A and one candidate for director of class B. The candidates so nominated shall be listed by the chairman indicating by whom nominated, and a copy of said list shall within 15 days after its completion be furnished by the chairman to each elector.

Every elector shall, within 15 days after the receipt of the said list, certify to the chairman his first, Second, and other choices of a director of class A and class B, respectively, upon a preferential ballot on a form furnished by the chairman of the board of directors of the Federal reserve bank of the district. Each elector shall make a cross opposite the name of the first, second and outer choices for a director of class A and for a director of class B, but shall not vote more than one choice for any one candidate.

Any candidate having a majority of all votes cast in the column of first choice shall be declared elected. If no candidate have a majority of all the votes in the first column then there shall be added together the votes cast by the electors for such candidates in the second column and the votes cast for the several candidates in the first column. If any candidate then have a majority of the electors voting, by adding together the first and second choices, he shall be declared elected. If no candidate have a majority of electors voting when the first and second choices shall have been added, then the votes cast in the third column for other choices shall be added together in like manner, and the candidate then having the highest number of votes shall be declared elected. An immediate report of election shall be declared.

Class C directors shall be appointed by the Federal reserve board. They shall have been for at least two years residents of the district for which they are appointed, one of whom shall be designated by said board as chairman of the board of directors of the Federal reserve bank and as "Federal reserve agent." He shall be a person of tested banking experience; and in addition to his duties as chairman of the board of directors of the Federal reserve bank, he shall be required to maintain under regulations to be established by the Federal reserve board a local office of said board on the premises of the Federal reserve bank. He shall make regular reports to the Federal reserve board, and shall act as its official representative for the performance of the functions conferred upon it by this act. He shall receive an annual compensation to be filed by the Federal reserve board and paid monthly by the Federal reserve bank to which he is designated. One of the directors of class C, who shall be a person of tested banking experience, shall be appointed by the Federal reserve board as deputy chairman and deputy Federal reserve agent to exercise the powers of the chairman of the board and Federal reserve agent in case of absence or disability of his principal.

Directors of Federal reserve banks shall receive, in addition to any compensation otherwise provided, a reasonable allowance for necessary expenses in attending meetings of their respective boards, which amount shall be paid by the respective Federal reserve banks, Any compensation that may be provided by boards of directors of Federal reserve banks for directors, officers or employees shall be subject to the approval of the Federal reserve board.

The reserve bank organization committee may, in organizing Federal reserve banks, call such meetings of bank directors in the several districts as may be necessary to carry out the purposes of this act, and may exercise the functions herein conferred upon the chairman of the board of directors of each Federal reserve bank pending the complete organization of such bank.

At the first meeting of the full board of directors of each Federal reserve bank, it shall be the duty of the directors of classes A, B and C, respectively, to designate one of the members of each class whose term of office shall expire in one year from the 1st of January nearest to date of such meeting, one whose term of office shall expire at the end of two years from said date, and one whose term of office shall expire at the end of three years from said date. Thereafter every director of a Federal reserve bank chosen as hereinbefore provided shall hold office for a term of three years. Vacancies that may occur in the several classes of directors of Federal reserve banks may be filled in the manner provided for the original selection of such directors, such appointees to hold office for the unexpired terms of their predecessors

Stock Issues; Increase And Decrease Of Capital

Sec. 5. The capital stock of each Federal reserve bank shall be divided into shares of $100 each. The outstanding capital stock shall be increased from time to time as member banks increase their capital stock and surplus or as additional banks become members and may be decreased as member banks reduce their capital stock or surplus or cease to be members. Shares of the capital stock of Federal reserve banks owned by member banks shall not be transferred or hypothecated. When a member bank increases its capital stock or surplus, it shall thereupon subscribe for an additional amount of capital stock of the Federal reserve bank of its district equal to 6 per cent of the said increase one-half of said subscription to be paid in the manner hereinbefore provided for original subscription and one-half subject to call of the Federal reserve board. A bank applying for stock in a Federal reserve bank at any time after the organization thereof must subscribe for an amount of the capital [Page 1433] stock of the Federal reserve bank equal to 6 per cent of the paid-up capital stock and surplus of said applicant bank, paying therefor its par value plus one-half of 1 per cent a month from the period of the last dividend. When the capital stock of any Federal reserve bank shall have been increased either on account of the increase of capital stock of member banks or on account of the increase in the number of member banks, the board of directors shall cause to be executed a certificate to the Comptroller of the Currency showing the increase in capital stock the amount paid in, and by whom paid When a member bank reduces its capital stock it shall surrender a proportionate amount of its holdings in the capital of said Federal reserve bank, and when a member bank voluntarily liquidates it shall surrender all of its holdings of the capital stock of said Federal reserve bank and be released from its stock subscription not previously called. In either case the shares surrendered shall be canceled and the member bank shall receive in payment therefor, under regulations to be prescribed by the Federal reserve board, a sum equal to its cash-paid subscriptions on the shares surrendered and one-half of 1 per cent a month from the period of the last dividend, not to exceed the bock value thereof, less any liability of such member bank to the Federal reserve bank

Sec. 6. If any member bank shall be declared insolvent and a receiver appointed therefor, the stock held by it in said Federal reserve bank shall be canceled, without impairment of its liability, and all cash-paid subscriptions on said stock, with one half of 1 per cent per month from the period of last dividend, not to exceed the book value thereof, shall be first applied to all debts of the insolvent member bank to the Federal reserve back, and the balance, if any, shall be paid to the receiver of the insolvent bank. Whenever the capital stock of a Federal reserve bank is reduced, either on account of a reduction in capital stock of any member bank or of the liquidation or insolvency of such bank, the board of directors shall cause to, be executed a certificate to the Comptroller of the Currency showing such reduction of capital stock and the amount repaid to such bank.

Division Of Earnings

Sec. 7. After all necessary expenses of a Federal reserve bank have been paid or provided for, the stockholders shall be entitled to receive an annual dividend of 6 per cent on the paid-in capital stock, which dividend shall be cumulative. After the aforesaid dividend claims have been fully met, all the net earnings shall be paid to the United States as a franchise tax, except that one-half of such net earnings shall be paid into a surplus fund until it shall amount to 40 per cent of the paid-in capital stock of such bank.

The net earnings derived by the United States from Federal reserve banks shall, in the discretion of the Secretary, be used to supplement the gold reserve held against outstanding United States notes, or shall be applied to the reduction of the outstanding bonded indebtedness of the United States under regulations to be prescribed by the Secretary of the Treasury. Should a Federal reserve bank be dissolved or go into liquidation any surplus remaining, after the payment of all debts, dividend requirements as hereinbefore provided, and the par value of the stock, shall be paid to and become the property of the United States and shall be similarly applied.

Federal reserve banks, including the capital stock and surplus therein and the income derived therefrom shall be exempt from Federal, State, and local taxation, except taxes upon real estate. [Emphasis added]

Sec. 8. Section 5154, United States Revised Statutes, is hereby amended to read as follows:

Any bank incorporated by special law of any State or of the United States or organized under the general laws of any State or of the United States and having an unimpaired capital sufficient to entitle it to become a national banking association under the provisions of the existing laws may, by the vote of the shareholders owning not less than 51 per cent of the capital stock of such bank or banking association, with the approval of the Comptroller of the Currency be converted into a national banking association with any name approved by the Comptroller of the Currency: *Provided, however,* That said conversion shall not be in contravention of the State law. In such case the articles of association and organization certificate may be executed by a majority of the directors of the bank or banking institution and the certificate shall declare that the owners of 51 per cent of the capital stock have authorized the directors to make such certificate, and to change or convert the bank or banking institution into a national association. A majority of the directors after executing the articles of association and the organization certificate shall have power to execute all other papers and to do whatever may be required to make its organization perfect and complete as a national association. The shares of any such bank may continue to be for the same amount each as they were before the conversion, and the directors may continue to be directors of the association until others are elected or appointed in accordance with the provisions of the statutes of the United States. When the comptroller has given to such bank or banking association a certificate that the provisions of this act have been complied with, such bank or banking association and all its stockholders, officers, :and employees, shall have the same powers and privileges, and shall be subject to the cane duties, liabilities, and regulations, in all respects, as shall have been prescribed by the Federal reserve act and by the national banking act for associations originally organized as national banking associations.

State Banks As Members

Sec. 9 Any bank incorporated by special law of any State, or organized under the general laws of any State or of the United States, may make application to the reserve bank organization committee, pending organization and thereafter to the Federal reserve board for the right to subscribe to the stock of the Federal reserve bank organized or to be organized within the Federal reserve district where the applicant is located. The organization committee or the Federal reserve board, under such rules and regulations as it may prescribe, subject to the provisions of this section may permit the applying bank to become a stockholder in the Federal reserve bank of the district in which the applying bank is located. Whenever the organization committee or the Federal reserve board shall permit the applying bank to become a stockholder in the Federal reserve bank of the district, stock shall be issued and paid for under the rules and regulations in this act provided for national banks which become stockholders in Federal reserve banks.

The organization committee or the Federal reserve board shall establish by-laws for the general government of its conduct in acting upon applications made by the State banks and banking associations and trust companies for stock ownership in Federal reserve banks. Such by-laws shall require applying banks not organized under Federal law to comply with the reserve and capital requirements and to submit to the examination and regulations prescribed by the organization committee or by the Federal reserve board. No applying bank shall be admitted to membership in a Federal reserve bank unless it possesses a paid-up unimpaired capital sufficient to entitle it to become a national banking association in the place where it is situated, under the provisions of the national banking act.

Amy bank becoming a member of a Federal reserve bank under the provisions of this section shall, in addition to the regulations and restrictions hereinbefore provided, be required to conform to the provisions of law imposed on the national banks respecting the limitation of liability which may be incurred by any person, firm, or corporation to such banks, the prohibition against making purchase of or loans on stock of such banks and the withdrawal or impairment of capital, or the payment of unearned dividends, and to such rules and regulations as the Federal reserve board may, in pursuance thereof, prescribe.

Such banks, and the officers agents, and employees thereof, shall also be subject to the provisions of and to the penalties prescribed by sections 5198 5200, 5201, and 5208, and 5209 of the Revised Statutes. The member banks shall also be required to make reports of the conditions and of the payments of dividends to the comptroller, as provided in sections 5211 and 5212 of the Revised Statutes, and shall be subject to the penalties prescribed by section 5213 for the failure to make such report.

If at any time it shall appear to the Federal reserve board that a member bank has failed to comply with the provisions of this section or the regulations of the Federal reserve board, it shall be, within the power of the said board, after hearing to require such bank to surrender its stock in the Federal reserve bank; upon such surrender the Federal reserve bank shall pay the cash paid subscriptions to the said stock with interest at the rate of one-half of 1 per cent per month, computed from the last dividend, if earned, not to exceed the book value thereof, less any liability to said Federal reserve bank, except the subscription liability not previously called, which shall be canceled, and said Federal reserve bank shall, upon notice from the Federal reserve board be required to suspend said bank from further privileges of membership and shall within 30 days of such notice cancel and retire its stock and make payment therefore in the manner herein provided. The Federal reserve board may restore membership upon due proof of compliance with the conditions imposed by this section.

Federal Reserve Board

Sec. 10. A Federal reserve board is hereby created which shall consist of seven members, including the Secretary of the Treasury and the Comptroller of the Currency, who shall be [Page 1434] members ex officio and five members appointed by the President of the United States, by and with the advice and consent of Senate. In selecting the five appointive members of the Federal reserve board, not more than one of whom shall be selected from any one Federal reserve district, the President shall have due regard to a fair representation of the different commercial, industrial, and geographical divisions of the country. The five members of the Federal reserve board appointed by the President and confirmed as aforesaid shall devote their entire time to the business of the. Federal reserve board and shall each receive an annual salary of $12,000 payable monthly together with actual necessary traveling expenses, and the Comptroller of the currency, as ex officio member of the Federal reserve board, shall, in addition to the salary now paid him as Comptroller of the Currency, receive the sum of $7,000 annually for his services as a member of said board.

The members of said board, the Secretary of the Treasury, the Assistant Secretaries of the Treasury, and the Comptroller of the Currency shall be ineligible during the time they are in office and for 2 years thereafter to hold any office, position, or employment in any member bank. Of the five members thus appointed by the President at least two shall be persons experienced in banking or finance. One shall be designated by the President to serve for 2, one for 4, one for 6, one for 8, and one for 10 years, and thereafter each member so appointed shall serve for a term of 10 years unless sooner removed for cause by the President. Of the five persons thus appointed, one shall be designated by the President as governor and one as vice governor of the Federal reserve board. The governor of the Federal reserve board, subject to its supervision shall be the active executive officer. The Secretary of the Treasury may assign offices in the Department of the Treasury for the use of the Federal reserve board. Each member of the Federal reserve board shall within 15 days after notice of appointment make and subscribe to the oath of office.

The Federal reserve board shall have power to levy semiannually upon the Federal reserve banks, in proportion to their capital stock and surplus, an assessment sufficient to pay its estimated expenses and the salaries of its members and employees for the half year succeeding the levying of such assessment together with any deficit carried forward from the preceding half year.

The first meeting of the Federal reserve board shall be held in Washington, D. C., as soon as may be after the passage of this act, at a date to be fixed by the reserve bank organization committee. The Secretary of the Treasury shall be ex officio chairman of the Federal reserve board. No member of the Federal reserve board shall be an officer or director of any bank, banking institution, trust company, or Federal reserve bank nor hold stock in any bank, banking institution or trust company; and before entering upon his duties as a member of the Federal reserve board he shall certify under oath to the Secretary of the Treasury that he has complied with this requirement. Whenever a vacancy shall occur, other than by expiration of term, among the five members of the Federal reserve board appointed by the President, as above provided a successor shall be appointed by the President, with the advice and consent of the senate, to fill such vacancy, and when appointed he shall hold office for the unexpired term of the member whose place he is selected to fill.

The President shall have power to fill all vacancies that may happen on the Federal reserve board during the recess of the senate by granting commissions which shall expire 30 days after the next session of the Senate convenes.

Nothing in this act contained shall be construed as taking away any powers heretofore vested by law in the Secretary of the Treasury which relate to the supervision management, and control of the Treasury Department and bureaus under such department and wherever any power vested by this act in the Federal reserve board or the Federal reserve agent appears to conflict with the powers of the Secretary of the Treasury, such powers shall be exercised subject to the supervision and control of the Secretary.

The Federal reserve board shall annually make a full report of its operations to the Speaker of the House of Representatives, who shall cause the same to be printed for the information of the Congress.

Section 324 of the Revised Statutes of the United States shall be amended so as to read as follows: There shall be in the Department of the Treasury a bureau charged with the execution of all laws passed by Congress relating to the issue and regulation of national currency secured by United States bonds, and, under the general supervision of the Federal reserve board of all Federal reserve notes, the chief officer of which bureau shall be called the Comptroller of the Currency and shall perform his duties under the general directions of the Secretary of the Treasury.

SEC. 11. The Federal reserve board shall be authorized ;and empowered:

(a) To examine at its discretion the accounts, books, and affairs of each Federal reserve bank and of each member bank and to require such statements and reports as it may deem necessary The said board shall publish once each week a statement showing the condition of each Federal reserve bank and a consolidated statement for all Federal reserve banks. Such statements shall show in detail the assets and liabilities of the Federal reserve banks, single and combined, and shall furnish full information regarding the character of the money held as reserve and the amount, nature, and maturities of the paper and other investments owned or held by Federal reserve banks.

(b) To permit, or, on the affirmative vote of at least five members of the reserve board, to require Federal reserve banks to rediscount the discounted paper of other Federal reserve banks at rates of interest to be fixed by the Federal reserve board.

(e) To suspend for a period not exceeding 30 days, and from time to time to renew such suspension for periods not exceeding 15 days, any reserve requirement specified in this act: Provided, That it shall establish a graduated tax upon the amounts by which the reserve requirements of this act may be permitted to fall below the level hereinafter specified: And provided further That when the old reserve held against Federal reserve notes falls below 40 per cent, the Federal reserve board shall establish a graduated tax of not more than 1 per cent per annum upon such deficiency until the reserves fall to 32.5

per cent, and when said reserve falls below 32 per cent, a tax at the rate increasingly of not less than 1.5 per cent per annum upon each 2.5 per cent or fraction thereof that such reserve falls below 32.5 per cent. The tax shall be paid by the reserve bank but the reserve bank shall add an amount equal to said tax to the rates of interest and discount fixed by the Federal reserve board.

(d) To supervise and regulate through the bureau under the charge of the Comptroller of the Currency the issue and retirement of Federal reserve notes, and to prescribe rules and regulations under which such notes may be delivered by the comptroller to the Federal reserve agents applying therefor.

(e) To add to the number of cities classified as reserve and central reserve cities under existing law in which national banking association are subject to the reserve requirements set forth in section 20 of this act; or to reclassify existing reserve and central reserve cities or to terminate their designation as such.

(f) To suspend or remove any officer or director of any Federal reserve bank, the cause of such removal to be forthwith communicated in writing by the Federal reserve board to the removed officer or director and to said bank.

(g) To require the writing off of doubtful or worthless assets upon the books and balance sheets of Federal reserve banks.

(h) To suspend, for the violation of any of the provisions of this act, the operations of any Federal reserve bans:, to take possession thereof, administer the same during the period of suspension and, when deemed advisable, to liquidate or reorganize such bank.

(i) To require bonds of Federal reserve agents, to make regulations for the safeguarding of all collateral, bonds, Federal reserve notes, money or property of any kind deposited in the hands of such agents, and said board shall perform the duties functions, or services specified in this act, and make all rules and regulations necessary to enable said board effectively to perform the same.

(j) To exercise general supervision over said Federal reserve banks.

(k) To grant by special permit to national banks applying therefor, when not in contravention of State or local law, the right to act as trustee, executor, administrator, or registrar of stocks and bonds under such rules and regulations as the said board may prescribe.

(l) To employ such attorneys, experts, assistants, clerks, or other employees as may he deemed necessary to conduct the business of the board. All salaries and fees shall be fixed in advance by said board and shall be paid in the same manner as the salaries of the members of said board. All such attorneys, experts, assistants, clerks, and other employees shall be appointed without regard to the provisions of the act of January 16, 1883 (Vol. 22 U. S. Stat. L.p. 403), and amendments thereto, or any rule or regulation made in pursuance thereof Provided, that nothing herein shall prevent the President from placing said employees in the classified service.

Federal Advisory Council

Sec. 12. There is hereby created a Federal advisory council, which shall consist of as many members as there are Federal reserve districts. Each Federal reserve bank by its board of [Page 1435] directors shall annually elect from its own Federal reserve district one member of said council, who shall receive such compensation and allowances as may be fixed by his board of directors subject to the approval of the Federal reserve board. The meetings of said advisory council shall be held at Washington D. C., at least four times each year, and oftener if called by the Federal reserve board. The council may in addition to the meetings above provided for hold such other meetings in Washington, D. C. or elsewhere, as it may deem necessary, may select its own officers and adopt its own methods of procedure, and a majority of its members shall constitute a quorum for the transaction of business. Vacancies in the council shall be filled by the respective reserve banks, and members selected to fill vacancies shall serve for the unexpired term.

The Federal advisory council shall have power by itself or through its officers, (1) to confer directly with the Federal reserve board on general business conditions; (2) to make oral or written representations concerning matters within the jurisdiction of said board; (3) to call for information and to make recommendations in regard to discount rates, rediscount business, note issues, reserve conditions in the various districts, the purchase and sale of gold or securities by reserve banks, open market operations by said banks, and the general affairs of the reserve banking system.

Powers Of Federal Reserve Banks

Sec. 13. Any Federal reserve bank may receive from any of its member banks, and from the United States, deposits of current funds in lawful money, national-bank notes, Federal reserve notes, or checks and drafts upon solvent member banks, payable upon presentation ; or, solely for exchange purposes, may receive from other Federal reserve banks deposits of current funds in lawful money, national-bank notes, or checks and drafts upon solvent member or other Federal reserve banks, payable upon presentation.

Upon the indorsement of any of its member banks, with a waiver of demand, notice and protest by such bank, any Federal reserve bank may discount notes, drafts, and bills of exchange arising out of actual commercial transactions; that is, notes, drafts, and bills of exchange issued or drawn for agricultural, industrial, or commercial purposes, or the proceeds of which have been used, or are to be used, for such purposes, the Federal reserve board to have the right to determine or define the character of the paper thus eligible for discount, within the meaning of this act. Nothing in this act contained shall be construed to prohibit such notes, drafts, and bills of exchange, secured by staple agricultural products, or other goods, wares, or merchandise from being eligible for such discount; but such definition shall not include notes, drafts, or bills covering merely investments or issued or drawn for the purpose of carrying or trading in stocks, bonds, or other investment securities, except bonds and notes of the Government of the United States. Notes, drafts, and bills admitted to discount under the terms of this paragraph must have a maturity at the time of discount of not more than 90 days: *Provided* That notes, drafts, and bills drawn or issued for agricultural purposes or based on lire stock and having a maturity not exceeding six months may be discounted in an amount to be limited to a percentage of the capital of the Federal reserve bank, to be ascertained and fixed by the Federal reserve board.

Any Federal reserve bank may discount acceptances which are based on the importation or exportation of goods and which have a maturity at time of discount of not more than three months, and indorsed by at least one member bank. The amount of acceptances so discounted shall at no time exceed one-half the paid-up capital stock; and surplus of the bank for which the rediscounts are made.

The aggregate of such notes and bills bearing the signature or indorsement of any one person, company, firm, or corporation rediscounted for any one bank shall at no time exceed 10 per cent of the unimpaired capital and surplus of said bank; but this restriction shall not apply to the discount of bills of exchange drawn in good faith against actually existing values.

Any member bank may accept drafts or bills of exchange drawn upon it and growing out of transactions involving the importation or exportation of goods having not more than six months sight to run; but no bank shall accept such bills to an amount equal at any time in the aggregate to more than one half its capital stock and surplus.

Section 5202 of the Revised Statutes of the United States is hereby amended so as to read as follows: No national banking association shall at any time he indebted, or in any way liable to an amount exceeding the amount of its capital stock at such time actually paid in and remaining undiminished by losses or otherwise, except on account of demands of the nature following:

First. Notes of circulation.

Second. Moneys deposited with or collected by the association.

Third. Bills of exchange or drafts drawn against money actually on deposit to the credit of the association, or due thereto.

Fourth. Liabilities to the stockholders of the association for dividends and reserve profits.

Fifth. Liabilities incurred under the provisions of the Federal reserve act.

The rediscount by any Federal reserve bank of any bills receivable and of domestic and foreign bills of exchange, and of acceptances authorized by this act, shall be subject to such restrictions, limitations, and regulations as may be imposed by the Federal reserve board.

Open Market Operations

Sec. 14. Any Federal reserve bank may, under rules and regulations prescribed by the Federal reserve board purchase and sell in the open market, at home or abroad, either from or to domestic or foreign banks, firms, corporations, or individuals, cable transfers and bankers' acceptances and bills of exchange of the kinds and maturities by this act made eligible for rediscount, with or without the indorsement of a member bank.

Every Federal reserve bank shall have power:

(a) To deal in gold coin and bullion at home or abroad, to make loans thereon, exchange Federal reserve notes for gold, gold coin, or gold certificates, and to contract for loans of gold coin or bullion giving therefor, when necessary, acceptable security, including the hypothecation of United States bonds or other securities which Federal reserve banks are authorized to hold ;

(b) To buy and sell, at home or abroad, bonds and notes of the United States, and bills, notes, revenue bonds, and warrants with a maturity from date of purchase of not exceeding six months, issued in anticipation of the collection of taxes or in anticipation of the receipt of assured revenues by any State, county, district, political subdivision or municipality in the continental United States, including irrigation, drainage and reclamation districts, such purchases to be made in accordance with rules and regulations prescribed by the Federal reserve board;

(c) To purchase from member banks and to sell, with or without its indorsement, bills of exchange arising out of commercial transactions actions, as hereinbefore defined;

(d) To establish from time to time, subject to review and determination of the Federal reserve board, rates of discount to be charged by the Federal reserve bank for each class of paper, which shall be fixed with a view of accommodating commerce and business;

(e) To establish accounts with other Federal reserve banks for exchange purposes and, with the consent of the Federal reserve board, to open and maintain banking accounts in foreign countries, appoint correspondents, and establish agencies in such countries wheresoever it may deem best for the purpose of purchasing, selling, and collecting bills of exchange, and to buy and sell with or without its indorsement, through such correspondents or agencies, bills of exchange arising out of actual commercial transactions which have not more than 90 days to run and which bear the signature of two or more responsible parties.

Government Deposits

Sec. 15. The moneys held in the general fund of the Treasury except the 5 per cent fund for the redemption of outstanding national-bank notes and the funds provided in this act for the redemption of Federal reserve notes may, upon the direction of the Secretary of the Treasury, be deposited in Federal reserve banks, which banks, when required by the Secretary of the Treasury, shall act as fiscal agents of the United States; and the revenues of the Government or any part thereof may be deposited in such banks and disbursements may be made by checks drawn against such deposits.

No public funds of the Philippine Islands, or of the postal savings, or any Government funds, shall be deposited in the continental United States in any bank not belonging to the system established by this act: *Provided*, however, That nothing in this act shall be construed to deny the right of the Secretary of the Treasury to use member banks as depositories.

Note Issues

Sec. 16. Federal reserve notes to be issued at the discretion of the Federal reserve board for the purpose of making advances to Federal reserve banks through the Federal reserve agents as hereinafter set forth and for no other purpose, are hereby authorized. The said notes shall be obligations of the United States and shall be receivable by all national and member banks and Federal reserve banks and for all taxes, customs, and other public dues, they, shall be redeemed in gold on [Page 1436] demand at the Treasury Department of the United States, in the city of

Washington D. C., or in gold or lawful money at any Federal reserve bank.

Any Federal reserve bank may make application to the local Federal reserve agent, for such amount of the Federal reserve notes hereinbefore provided for as it may require. Such application shall be accompanied with a tender to the local Federal reserve agent of collateral in amount equal to the sum of the Federal reserve notes thus applied for and issued pursuant to such application. The collateral security thus offered shall be notes and bills, accepted for rediscount under the provisions of section 13 of this act, and the Federal reserve agent shall each day notify the Federal reserve board of all issues and withdrawals of Federal reserve notes to and by the Federal reserve bank to which he is accredited. The said Federal reserve board may at any time call upon a Federal reserve bask for additional security to protect the Federal reserve notes issued to it.

Every Federal reserve bank shall maintain reserves in gold or lawful money of not less than 35 per cent against its deposits and reserves in gold of not less than 40 per cent against its Federal reserve notes in actual circulation and not offset by gold or lawful money deposited with the Federal reserve agent. Notes so paid out shall bear upon their faces a distinctive letter and serial number, which shall be assigned by the Federal reserve board to each Federal reserve bank Whenever Federal reserve notes issued through one Federal reserve bank shall be received by another Federal reserve bank they shall be promptly returned for credit or redemption to the Federal reserve bank though which they were originally issued. No Federal reserve bank shall pay out notes issued through another under penalty of a tax of 10 per cent upon the face value of notes so paid out. Notes presented for redemption at the Treasury of the United States shall be paid out of the redemption fund and returned to the Federal reserve banks through which they were originally issued, and thereupon such Federal reserve bank shall, upon demand of the Secretary of the Treasury, reimburse such redemption fund in lawful money or, if such Federal reserve notes have been redeemed by the Treasurer in gold or gold certificates, then such funds shall be reimbursed to the extent deemed necessary by the Secretary of the Treasury in gold or gold certificates, and such Federal reserve bank shall, so long as any of its Federal reserve notes remain outstanding, maintain with the Treasurer in gold an amount sufficient in the judgment of the secretary to provide for all redemptions to be made by the Treasurer. Federal reserve notes received by the Treasury, otherwise than for redemption, may be exchanged for gold out of the redemption fund hereinafter provided and returned to the reserve bank through which they were originally issued, or they may be returned to such bank for the credit of the United States. Federal reserve notes unfit for circulation shall be returned by the Federal reserve agents to the Comptroller of the Currency for cancellation and destruction.

The Federal reserve board shall require each Federal reserve bank to maintain on deposit in the Treasury of the United States a sum in gold sufficient in the judgment of the Secretary of the Treasury for the redemption of the Federal reserve notes issued to such bank, but in no event less than 5 per cent; but such deposit of gold shall be counted and included as part of the 40 per cent reserve hereinbefore required. The board shall have the right, acting through the Federal reserve agent, to grant in whole or in part or to reject entirely the application of any Federal reserve bank for Federal reserve notes; but to the extent that such application may be granted, the Federal reserve board shall, through its local Federal reserve agent, supply Federal reserve notes to the bank so applying and such bank shall be charged with the amount of such notes and shall pay such rate of interest on said amount as may be established by the Federal reserve board, and the amount of such Federal reserve notes so issued to any such bank shall, upon delivery, together with such notes of such Federal reserve bank as may be issued under section 18 of this act upon security of United States 2 per cent Government bonds, became a first and paramount lien on all the assets of such bank.

Any Federal reserve bank may at any time reduce its liability for outstanding Federal reserve notes by depositing, with the Federal reserve agent, its Federal reserve notes, gold, gold certificates, or lawful money of the United States. Federal reserve notes so deposited shall not be reissued, except upon compliance with the conditions of an original issue.

The Federal reserve agent shall hold such gold, gold certificates or lawful money available exclusively for exchange for the outstanding Federal reserve notes when offered by the reserve bank of which he is a director. Upon the request of the Secretary of the Treasury the Federal reserve board shall require the Federal reserve agent to transmit so much of said gold to the Treasury of the United States as may be required for the exclusive purpose of the redemption of such notes.

Any Federal reserve bank may at its discretion withdraw collateral deposited with the local Federal reserve agent for the protection of its Federal reserve notes deposited with it and shall at the same time substitute therefor other like collateral of equal amount with the approval of the Federal reserve agent under regulations to be prescribed by the Federal reserve board.

In order to furnish suitable notes for circulation as Federal reserve notes, the Comptroller of the Currency shall, under the direction of the Secretary of the Treasury cause plates and dies to be engraved in the best manner to guard against counterfeits and fraudulent alterations, and shall have printed therefrom and numbered such quantities of such notes of the denominations of $5, $10, $20, $50, $100, as may be required to supply the Federal reserve banks. Such notes shall be in form and tenor as directed by the Secretary of the Treasury under the provisions of this act and shall bear the distinctive numbers of the several Federal reserve banks through which they are issued.

When such notes have been prepared, they shall be deposited in the Treasury or in the subtreasury or mint of the United States nearest the place of business of each Federal reserve bank and shall be held for the use of such bank subject to the order of the Comptroller of the Currency for their delivery, as provided by this act.

The plates and dies to be procured by the Comptroller of the Currency for the printing of such circulating notes shall remain under his control and direction, and the expenses necessarily incurred in executing the laws relating to the procuring of such notes, and all other expenses incidental to their issue and retirement, shall be paid by the Federal reserve banks, and the Federal reserve board shall include in its estimate of expenses levied against the Federal reserve banks a sufficient amount to cover the expenses herein provided for.

The examination of plates, dies, bed pieces, etc., and regulations relating to such examination of plates, dies, etc., of national-bank notes provided for in section 5174 Revised Statutes, is hereby extended to include notes herein provided for.

Any appropriation heretofore made out of the general funds of the Treasury for engraving plates and dies, the purchase of distinctive paper, or to cover any other expense in connection with the printing of national-bank notes or notes provided for by the act of May 30, 1908, and any distinctive paper that may be on hand at the time of the passage of this act may be used in the discretion of the Secretary for the purposes of this act, and should the appropriations heretofore made be insufficient to meet the requirements of this act in addition to circulating notes provided for by existing law, the Secretary is hereby authorized to use so much of any funds in the Treasury not otherwise appropriated for the purpose of furnishing the notes aforesaid: *Provided*, however, That nothing in this section contained shall be construed as exempting national banks or Federal reserve banks from their liability to reimburse the United States for any expenses incurred in printing and issuing circulating notes.

Every Federal reserve bank shall receive on deposit at par from member banks or from Federal reserve banks checks and drafts drawn upon any of its depositors, and when remitted by a Federal reserve bank, checks and drafts drawn by any depositor in any other Federal reserve bank or member bank upon funds to the credit of said depositor in said reserve bank or member bank. Nothing herein contained shall be construed as prohibiting a member bank from charging its actual expense incurred in collecting and remitting funds, or for exchange sold to its patrons. The Federal reserve board shall, by rule, fix the charges to be collected by the member banks from its patrons whose checks are cleared through the Federal reserve bank and the charge which may be imposed for the service of clearing or collection rendered by the Federal reserve bank.

The Federal reserve board shall make and promulgate from time to time regulations governing the transfer of funds and charges therefor among Federal reserve banks and their branches and may at its discretion exercise the functions of a clearing house for such Federal reserve banks or may designate a Federal reserve bank to exercise such functions, and may also require each such bank to exercise the functions of a clearing house for its member banks.

Sec. 17. So much of the provisions of section 5159 of the Revised Statutes of the United States and section 4 of the act of June 20, 9571, and section 8 of the act of July 12, 1882 and of any other provisions of existing statutes as require that before any national banking association shall be authorized to [Page 1437] commence banking business, it shall transfer and deliver to the Treasurer of the United States a stated amount of United States registered bonds is hereby repealed.

Refunding Bonds

Sec. 18. After two years From the passage of this act, and at any time during a period of 20 years thereafter any member bank desiring to retire the whole or any part of its circulating notes may file with the Treasurer of the United States an application to sell for its account at par and accrued interest, United States bond securing circulation to be retired.

The Treasurer shall, at the end of each quarterly period, furnish the Federal reserve board with a list of such applications, and the Federal reserve board may, in its discretion, require the Federal reserve banks to purchase such bonds from the banks whose applications have been filed with the Treasurer at least 10 days before the end of any quarterly period at which the Federal reserve board may direct the purchase to be made: *Provided*, That Federal reserve banks shall not be permitted to purchase an amount to exceed $25,000,000 of such bonds in any one year, and which amount shall include bonds acquired under section 4 of this act by the Federal reserve bank: *Provided*, further, That the Federal reserve board shall allot to each Federal reserve bank such proportion of such bonds as the capital and surplus of such bank shall bear to the aggregate capital and surplus of all the Federal reserve banks.

Upon notice from the Treasurer of the amount of bonds so sold for its account, each member bank shall duly assign and transfer, in writing, such bonds to the Federal reserve bank purchasing the same, and such Federal reserve bank shall, thereupon, deposit lawful money with the Treasurer of the United States for the purchase price of such bonds, and the Treasurer shall pay to the member bank; selling such bonds any balance due after deducting a sufficient sum to redeem its outstanding notes secured by such bonds, which notes shall be canceled and permanently retired when redeemed.

The Federal reserve banks purchasing such bonds shall be permitted to take out an amount of circulating notes equal to the Par value of such bonds.

Upon the deposit with the Treasurer of the United States of bonds so purchased, or any bonds with the circulating privilege acquired under section 4 of this act, any Federal reserve bans; making such deposit in the manner provided by existing law, shall be entitled to receive from the Comptroller of the Currency circulating notes in blank, registered and countersigned as provided by law, equal in amount to the par value of the bonds so deposited. Such notes shall be the obligations of the Federal reserve bank procuring the same, and shall be in form prescribed by the Secretary of the Treasury, and to the same tenor and effect as national-bank notes now provided by law. They shall be issued and redeemed under the same terms and conditions as national-bank notes except that they shall not be limited to the amount of the capital stock of the Federal reserve bank issuing them.

Upon application of any Federal reserve bank, approved by the Federal reserve board, the Secretary of the Treasury may issue, in exchange for United States 2 per cent gold bonds bearing the circulation privilege, but against which no circulation is outstanding, 1-year gold notes of the United States without the circulation privilege, to an amount not to exceed one-half of the 2 per cent bonds so tendered for exchange, and 30-year 3 per cent gold bonds without the circulation privilege for the remainder of the 2 per cent bonds so tendered: *Provided*, That at the time of such exchange the Federal reserve bank obtaining such 1-year gold notes shall enter into an obligation with the Secretary of the Treasury binding itself to purchase from the United States for gold at the maturity of such 1-year note, an amount equal to those delivered in exchange for such bonds, if so requested by the Secretary, and at each maturity of 1-year notes so purchased by such Federal reserve bank to purchase from the United States such an amount of 1-year notes as the Secretary may tender to such bank, not to exceed the amount issued to such bank in the first instance, in exchange for the 2 per cent United States gold bonds; said obligation to purchase at maturity such notes shall continue in force for a period not to exceed 30 years.

For the purpose of making the exchange herein provided for, the Secretary of the Treasury is authorized to issue at par Treasury notes in coupon or registered form as he may prescribe in denominations of $100 or any multiple thereof, bearing interest at the rate of 3 per cent per annum, payable quarterly, such Treasury notes to be payable not more than 1 year from the date of their issue in gold coin of the present standard value and to be exempt as to principal and interest from the payment of all taxes and duties of the United States except as provided by this act as well as from taxes in any form by or under State, municipal, or local authorities. And for the same purpose, the Secretary is authorized and empowered to issue United States gold bonds at par, bearing 3 per cent interest payable 30 years from date of issue, such bonds to be of the same several tenor and effect and to be issued under the same general terms and conditions as the United States 3 per cent bonds without the circulation privilege now issued and outstanding.

Upon application of any Federal reserve bank, approved by the Federal reserve board, the Secretary may issue at par such 3 per cent bonds in exchange for the 1-year gold notes herein provided for.

Bank Reserves

Sec. 19. Demand deposits within the meaning of this act shall comprise all deposits payable within 30 days, and time deposits shall comprise all deposits payable after 30 days, and all savings accounts and certificates of deposit which are subject to not less than 30 days notice before payment.

When the Secretary of the Treasury shall have officially announced in such manner as he may elect, the establishment of a Federal reserve bank in any district, every subscribing member bank shall establish and maintain reserves as follows:

(a) A bank not in a reserve or central reserve city as now or hereafter defined shall hold and maintain reserves equal to 12 per cent of the aggregate amount of its demand deposits and 5 per cent of its time deposits, as follows:

In its vaults for a period of 36 months after said date five-twelfths thereof and permanently thereafter four-twelfths.

In the Federal reserve bank of its district, for a period of 12 months after said date, two-twelfths, and for each succeeding 6 months an additional one-twelfth, until five-twelfths have been so deposited which shall be the amount permanently required.

For a period of 36 months after said date the balance of the reserves may be held in its own vaults, or in the: Federal reserve bank, or in national banks in reserve or central reserve cities as now defined by law.

After said 36 months period all of said reserves, except those hereinbefore required to be held in the vaults of the member bank and in the Federal reserve bank, shall be held in the vaults of the member bank or in the Federal reserve bank, or in both, at the option of the member bank.

(b) A bank in a reserve city, as now or hereafter defined shall hold and maintain reserves equal to 18 per cent of the aggregate amount of its demand deposits and 5 per cent of its time deposits, as follows:

In its vaults for a period of 36 months after said date six-fifteenths thereof, and permanently thereafter five-fifteenths. In the Federal reserve bank of its district for a period of 12 months after the date aforesaid at least three-fifteenths, and for each succeeding 6 months an additional one-fifteenth, until six-fifteenths have been so deposited, which shall be the amount permanently required.

For a period of 36 months after said date the balance of the reserves may be held in its own vaults, or in the Federal reserve bank, or in national banks in reserve or central reserve cities as now defined by law.

After said 36 months period all of said reserves, except those hereinbefore required to be held permanently in the vaults of the member bank, and in the Federal reserve bank, shall be held in its vaults or in the Federal reserve bank, or in both, at the option of the member bank.

(c) **A bank in a central reserve city, as now or hereafter defined, shall hold and maintain a reserve equal to 18 per cent of the aggregate amount of its demand deposits and 5 per cent of its time deposits, as follows:**

In its vaults six-eighteenths thereof.

In the Federal reserve bank seven-eighteenths.

The balance of said reserves shall be held in its own vaults or in the Federal reserve bank, at its option.

Any Federal reserve bank may receive from the member banks as reserves, not exceeding one-half of each installment, eligible paper as described in section 14 properly indorsed and acceptable to the said reserve bank.

If a State bank or trust company is required by the law of its State to keep its reserves either in its own vaults or with another State bank or trust company such reserve deposits so kept in such State bank or trust company shall he construed, within the meaning of this section as if they were reserve deposits in a national bank in a reserve or central reserve city for a period of three years after the Secretary of the Treasury shall have officially announced the establishment of a Federal reserve bank in the district in which such State bank or trust company is situate. Except as thus provided, no member bank shall keep on deposit with any nonmember bank a sum in excess of 10 per cent of its own paid -up capital and surplus. No [Page 1438] member bank shall act as the medium or agent of a nonmember Bank in applying for or receiving discounts from a Federal reserve bank under the provisions of this act except by permission of the Federal reserve board.

The reserve carried by a member bank with a Federal reserve bank may, under the regulations and subject to such penalties as may be prescribed by the Federal reserve board be checked against and withdrawn by such member bank for the purpose of meeting existing liabilities: *Provided, however,* That no bank shall at any time make new loans or shall pay any dividends unless and until the total reserve required by law is fully restored.

In estimating the reserves required by this act, the net balance of amounts due do and from other banks shall be taken as the basis for ascertaining the deposits against which reserves shall be determined. Balances in reserve banks due to member banks shall to the extent herein provided, be counted as reserves.

National banks located in Alaska or outside the continental United States may remain nonmember banks, and shall in that event maintain reserves and comply with all the conditions now provided by law regulating them; or said banks, except in the Philippine Islands, may, with the consent of the reserve board, become member banks of any one of the reserve districts, and shall, in that event, take stock, maintain reserves, and be subject to all the other provisions of this act.

SEC. 20. So much of sections 2 and 3 of the act of June 20, 1874, entitled "An act fixing the amount of United States notes, providing for a redistribution of the national-Bank currency, and for other purposes," as provides that the fund deposited by any national banking association with the Treasurer of the United States for the redemption of its notes shall be counted as a part of its lawful reserve as provided in the act aforesaid, is hereby repealed. And from and after the passage of this act such fund of 5 per cent shall in no case be counted by any national banking association as a part of its lawful reserve.

Bank Examinations

Sec. 21. Section 5240, United States Revised Statutes, is amended to read as follows:

> The Comptroller of the Currency-, with the approval of the Secretary of the Treasury, shall appoint examiners who shall examine every member bank at least twice in each calendar year and oftener if considered necessary: *Provided, however,* That the Federal reserve board may authorize examination by the State authorities to be accepted in the case of State banks and trust companies and may at any time direct the holding of a special examination of State banks or trust companies that are stockholders in any Federal reserve bank. The examiner making the examination of any national bank, or of any other member bank, shall have power to make a thorough examination of all the affairs of the bank and in doing so he shall have power to administer oaths and to examine any of the officers and agents thereof under oath and shall make a full and detailed report of the condition of said bank to the Comptroller of the Currency.

The Federal reserve board, upon the recommendation of the Comptroller of the Currency, shall fix the salaries of all bank examiners and make report thereof to Congress. The expense of the examinations herein provided for shall be assessed by the Comptroller of the Currency upon the banks examined in proportion to assets or resources held by the backs upon the dates of examination of the various banks.

In addition to the examinations made and conducted by the Comptroller of the Currency, every Federal reserve bank may, with the approval of the Federal reserve agent or the Federal reserve board, provide for special examination of member banks within its district.

The expense of such examinations shall be borne by the bank examined. Such examinations shall be so conducted as to inform the Federal reserve bank of the condition of its member banks and of the lines of credit which are being extended by them. Every Federal reserve bank shall at all times furnish to the Federal reserve board such information as may be demanded concerning the condition of any member bank within the district of the said Federal reserve bank.

No bank shall be subject to any visitatorial powers other than such as are authorized by law, or vested in the courts of justice or such as shall be or shall have been exercised or directed by Congress or by either house thereof or by any committee of Congress or of either house duly authorized.

The Federal reserve board shall, at least once each year, order an examination of each Federal reserve bank, and upon joint application of 10 member banks the Federal reserve board shall order a special examination and report of the condition of any Federal reserve bank.

Sec. 22. No member bank or any officer, director, or employee thereof shall hereafter make any loan or grant any gratuity to any bank examiner. Any bank officer, director, or employee violating this provision shall be deemed guilty of a misdemeanor and shall be imprisoned not exceeding one year or fined not more than $5,000, or both; and may be fined a further sum equal to the money so loaned or gratuity given. Any examiner accepting a loan or gratuity from any bank examined by him or from an officer, director, or employee thereof shall be deemed guilty of a misdemeanor and shall be imprisoned not exceeding one year or fined not more than $5,000, or both; and may be fined a further sum equal to the money so loaned or gratuity given; and shall forever thereafter be disqualified from holding office as a national-bank examiner. No national-bank examiner shall perform any other service for compensation while holding such office for any bank or officer, director, or employee thereof.

Other than the usual salary or director's fee paid to any officer, director, or employee of a member bank and other than a reasonable fee paid by said bank to such officer, director, or employee for services rendered to such bank, no officer, director, employee, or attorney of a member bank stall be a beneficiary of, or receive, directly or indirectly, any fee, commission, gift, or other consideration for or in connection with any transaction or business of the bank. No examiner, public or private, shall disclose the names of borrowers or the collateral for loans of a member bank to other than the proper officer of such bank without first having obtained the express permission in writing from the Comptroller of the Currency, or from the board of directors of such bank, except when ordered to do so by a court of competent jurisdiction or by direction of the Congress of the United States, or of either House thereof, or any committee of Congress or of either House duly authorized. Any person violating any provision of this section shall be punished by a fine of not exceeding $5,000 or by imprisonment not exceeding one year, or both.

Except as provided in existing laws, this provision shall not take effect until 60 days after the passage of this act.

Sec. 23. The stockholders of every national banking association shall be held individually responsible for all contracts, debts, and engagements of such association, each to the amount of his stock therein at the par value thereof in addition to the amount invested in such stock. The stockholders in any national banking association who shall have transferred their shares or registered the transfer thereof within 60 days next before the date of the failure of such association to meet its obligations, or with knowledge of such impending failure, shall be liable to the same extent as if they had made no such transfer, to the extent that the subsequent transferee fails to meet such liability; but this provision shall not be construed to affect in any way any recourse which such shareholders might otherwise have against those in whose names such shares are registered at the time of such failure.

Loans On Farm Lands

Sec. 24. Any national banking association not situated in a central reserve city may make loans secured by improved and unencumbered farm land, situated within its Federal reserve district, but no such loan shall be made for a longer time than five years, nor for an amount exceeding 50 per cent of the actual value of the property offered as security. Any such bank may make such locus in an aggregate sum equal to 25 per cent of its capital and surplus or to one-third of its time deposits; and such banks may continue hereafter as heretofore to receive time deposits and to pay interest on the same.

The Federal reserve board shall have power from time to time to add to the list of cities in which national banks stall not be permitted to make loans secured upon real estate in the manner described in this section.

Foreign Branches

Sec. 25. Any national banking association possessing a capitol and surplus of $1,000,000 or more may file application with the Federal reserve board, upon such conditions and under such regulations as may be prescribed by the said board, for the purpose of securing authority to establish branches in foreign countries or dependencies of the United States for the furtherance of the foreign commerce of the United States, and to act if required to do so, as fiscal agents of the United States. Such application shall specify, in addition to the name and capital of the banking association filing it, the place or places where the banking operation proposed are to be carried on, and the amount of capital set aside for the conduct of its foreign business The Federal reserve board shall have power to approve or to reject such application if, in its judgement, the amount of capital proposed to be set aside for the conduct of foreign business is inadequate, or if for other reasons the granting of such application is deemed inexpedient. [Page 1439]

Every national banking association which shall receive authority to establish foreign branches shall be required at all times to furnish information concerning the condition of such branches to the Comptroller of the Currency upon demand, and the Federal reserve board may order special examinations of the said foreign branches at such time or times as it may deem best. Every such national banking association shall conduct the accounts of each foreign branch independently of the accounts of other foreign branches established by it and of its home office, and shall at the end of each fiscal period transfer to its general ledger the profit or loss accruing at each branch as a separate item.

Sec. 26. All provisions of law inconsistent with or superceded by any of the provisions of this act are to that extent and to that extent only hereby repealed: *Provided*, Nothing in this act contained shall be construed to repeal the parity provision or provisions contained in an act approved March 14, 1900 entitled "An act to define and fix the standard of value, to maintain the parity of all forms of money issued or coined by the United States, to refund the public debt, and for other purposes," and the Secretary of the Treasury may for the purpose of maintaining such parity and to strengthen the gold reserve, borrow gold on the security of United States bonds authorized by section 2 of the act last referred to or for one year gold notes bearing interest at a rate of not to exceed 3 per cent per annum, or sell the same if necessary to obtain gold. When the funds of the Treasury on band justify, he may purchase and retire such outstanding bonds and notes.

SEC. 27. The provisions of the act of May 30, 1908, authorizing national currency associations, the issue of additional national-bank circulation and creating a National Monetary Commission, which expires by limitation under the terms of such act on the 30th day of June, 1914, are hereby extended to June 30, 1915, and sections 5153, 5172, 5191, and 5214 of the Revised Statutes of the United States, which were amended by the act of May 30, 1908, are hereby reenacted to read as such sections read prior to May 30, 1305, subject to such amendments or modifications as are prescribed in this act: *Provided, however*, That section 9 of the act first referred to in this section is hereby amended so as to change the tax rates fixed in said act by making the portion applicable thereto read as follows:

National banking associations having circulating notes secured otherwise than by bonds of the United States, shall pay for the first three months a tax at the rate of 3 per cent per annum upon the average amount of such of their notes in circulation as are based upon the deposit of such securities, and afterwards an additional tax rate of one-half of 1 per cent per annum for each month until a tax of 6 per cent per annum is reached and thereafter such tax of 6 per cent per annum upon the average amount of such notes.

SEC. 28. Section 5113 of the Revised Statutes is hereby amended and reenacted to read as follows: Any association formed under this title may by the vote of shareholders owning two-thirds of its capital stock, reduce its capital to any sum not below the amount required by this title to authorize the formation of associations; but no such reduction shall be allowable which will reduce the capital of the association below the amount required for its outstanding circulation, nor shall any reduction be made until the amount of the proposed reduction has been reported to the Comptroller of the Currency and such reduction has been approved by the said Comptroller of the Currency and by the Federal reserve board, or by the organization committee pending the organization of the Federal reserve board.

Sec. 29. If any clause, sentence, paragraph, or part of this act shall for any reason be adjudged by any court of competent jurisdiction to be invalid, such judgment shall not affect, impair, or invalidate the remainder of this act, but shall be confined in its operation to the clause, sentence, paragraph, of part thereof directly involved in the controversy in which such judgment shall have been rendered.

Sec. 30. The right to amend, alter, or repeal this act is hereby expressly reserved.

Carter Glass,
Charles A Korbly,

Managers on the part of the House.

Robt. L. Owen,
J. A. O'Gorman,
Jas. A. Reed,
Atlee Pomerene,
J. F. Shafroth,
Henry F. Hollis,

Managers on the part of the Senate.

The statement is as follows:

Statement

The managers on the part of the house at the conference on the disagreeing vote of the two Houses on the amendment of the Senate to the bill H. R. 7837 entitled "An act to provide for the establishment of Federal reserve banks, to furnish an elastic currency, to afford means of rediscounting commercial paper, to establish a more effective supervision of banking in the United States, and for other purposes," submit the following statement:

The House receded from its disagreement to the amendment of the Senate to the House bill with certain amendments, which are more specifically shown in Senate Document No. 335, Sixty-third Congress, second session a copy of which is attached hereto and which shows the House bill as it passed the House of Representatives, as amended by the Senate, and as agreed to in conference. The column in this document containing the bill as agreed to in conference shows by brackets and bold-face type that portion of the Senate amendment which was stricken out and the parts inserted by the House managers, respectively.

Carter Glass,
Charles A Korbly,

Managers on the part of the House.

The SPEAKER. The gentleman from Virginia is recognized for an hour.

[Omitted]

The SPEAKER. The gentleman from Virginia [Mr. Glass] asks unanimous consent that this debate shall be limited to 2 hours and 40 minutes, an hour and twenty minutes to be controlled by him, 1 hour by the gentleman from California [Mr. Hayes], and 20 minutes by the gentleman from Minnesota [Mr. Lindbergh]. Is there objection?

Mr. FOWLER. Mr. Speaker, reserving the right to object, I desire to inquire what arrangement will be made for extending remarks in the Record?

Mr. MANN. It has been granted to everybody.

Mr. RAGSDALE. Five days in which leave is granted to extend remarks.

[Omitted]

[Page 1445]

Mr. MOORE. [continued]

The Democratic caucus considers a bill in secret session for several months. The Representatives of a majority of the people have no voice in its preparation. It is brought into the House and passed in a day. The Senate receives the bill, and the Democratic Representatives ponder over it for months. It is forced through the Senate and returns to the House so changed in form that even the Democratic committee chairman of the House declares that if passed it will result in a veritable "saturnalia of inflation." In 40 minutes, less time than it takes to read the bill, the House is allowed to consider it. Then it goes to conference. And the people whose money is at stake are "in the saddle" and "popular rule" is supreme. Let us see.

The Senate appoints nine conferees to meet three conferees of the House and adjust the differences between the two bodies. When they get into action, the nine "popular-rule" Senate conferees are boiled down to six Democrats. The three "popular rule" conferees of the House are reduced to two Democrats. All Republicans are excluded from the conference. "Popular rule" now rests with the six Senators and the two little giants of the House—the gentleman from Virginia [Mr. Glass] and the gentleman from Indiana [Mr. Korbly].

Mr. GLASS. We confess.

Mr. MOORE. You are entitled to do so.

The bill is now brought back to the House in a 58-page document in triple columns and a 30-page closely printed report, which the House is to accept after two hours' discussion in order that the President and the Members may go off on their holiday vacations. And what is the principal change we are to vote upon after the two hours' discussion? On page 24 of the comparative print we find that "popular rule" in the steel-bound Democratic conference has restored to the President, as one of his Federal reserve board, the Comptroller of the Currency, whom he was in danger of losing under the Senate bill. Only one of the seven members of the Federal reserve board will go out of office during the President's term. Will the six others stand by the President and his Secretary of the Treasury against any order given by the President? If he plays politics to perpetuate his power, will they resist him?

Therefore the popular rule which Andrew Jackson strove for against the rule of Nicholas Biddle, of the United States Bank, is overthrown by the Democratic Party and the President becomes the absolute dictator of the public and private resources of the country which find their way into the national banks under the new system. Such tremendous power for good or ill was never granted to any President, nor has so great an inducement to perpetuate the power of any party been vouchsafed to any man in the history of this country.

This bill, apart from its many danger points and imperfections, is a travesty upon Democracy's so-called "popular rule." It is a confession of dictation and absolutism the like of which has no parallel in American annals.

Mr. HAYES. Mr. Speaker, I yield five minutes to the gentleman from New York [Mr. Platt].

Mr. PLATT. Mr. Speaker, it has been well said by the gentleman from Virginia [Mr. Glass] and by others that this is a great measure-one of the greatest measures that has passed this House of Representatives and the Congress of the United States for a long time. I want to congratulate my Democratic friends for the large measure of success they have attained in making the measure largely a good measure, but at the same time I want to point out to them that they are enacting this great measure with some very serious defects. and with a certain amount of fear and trembling, under the party lash and under threat from the President that there would be no Christmas dinners unless it was passed at once. And yet what have you done, gentlemen? You are passing a great measure which the Demoncratic Party is going to take credit for and on the end of it you are extending a Republican measure which you have condemned in most unmeasured terms on the floor of this House. There is nothing you have condemned more roundly and vehemently than the Vreeland-Aldrich law. It has been cursed from one end of this Hall to the other by gentlemen on the other side of the House. and yet this bill extends it for one year because our Democratic friends are afraid this bill may not be panic proof.

MR. GLASS. May I interrupt my colleague?

MR. PLATT. Certainly.

Mr. GLASS. Is it not fair to state that while we are extending the Vreeland-Aldrich Act we are amending it so as to make it available to the people of the country'? We reduce the tax, so the people may get the currency should they need it. [Applause on the Democratic side.]

MR. PLATT. Oh, I :admit you are making it more available, but at the same time it is a Republican measure which you have very much condemned, but you found it necessary to put it into this bill.

MR. GLASS. As a Republican measure it was not operative; as a Democratic measure it may be operative. [Applause on the Democratic side.]

MR. PLATT. Well, I hope it will not be needed, but there is a good deal in this bill based on the Vreeland-Aldrich bill besides, and that is one trouble with it. [Laughter.] The currency feature of this bill is a scheme whereby the United States issues notes for the banks. **It provides for a currency made to loan to the banks at a low rate of interest, and that appears as a tremendous special privilege given to privately controlled banking institutions. Other organizations of the country, like the farmers and workingmen, will ask why, if the United States can issue its Treasury note, to loan to banks at one-half of 1 per cent interest, it can not issue notes to loan to them at 2 per cent.** And it is a perfectly logical conclusion that is going to give you a whole lot of trouble. I agree with everything that my colleague the gentleman from California [Mr. Hayes] has said-that the notes issued under this bill ought to be bank notes. The banks are to keep the reserves and can redeem them, but for some reason unknown, or perhaps not entirely unknown you have characterized these notes as Government notes when really they are practically bank notes and —

Mr. GLASS. I will ask the gentleman if, under the national bank act. a distinctly Republican measure, you have not been loaning currency to the banks for 50 years on their collateral, while not loaning to farmers? [Applause on the Democratic side.]

Mr. PLATT. No; we hare not. We have been depositing money and taking security for it. You can call that a loan if you want to, but it is a deposit. Under this bill the Government lends its notes to the banks at a low rate of interest and the banks loan the same notes to the people at a high rate of interest, and this is a special privilege.

MR. KORBLY. Is it not a fact that the banks put up 140 per cent of security to get these borrowed notes you speak of?

Mr. PLATT. I thick they are secured sufficiently. I agree with the gentleman from Virginia and the gentleman from Indiana, in that the notes are probably secure, but you Dave got to explain from now on what business they have to read as Government notes when they ought to be bank notes standing on the security of good banking and a sufficient rescue.[applause.]

The Speaker. The time of the gentleman from New York has expired.

The gentleman from Minnesota [Mr. Lindbergh] is recognized.

Mr. LINDBERGH. Mr. Speaker, I am mindful of a picture in life. It is that of the school children of today, throughout all parts of this country, being taught the principles of conservation — told that it is not their generation alone to conserve for, but that they must build for all the future as well; told to conserve the forests, the minerals, the waters, the soils, and all the things required for the use of humanity. This is being taught in all the schools and the homes. For example:

Nevis is a small village located in one of nature's beautiful parks in northern Minnesota. In the early summer I accepted an invitation to address the people at a fair which was held at Nevis last October. You Democrats issued one of your caucus decrees to put the House out of work just previous, therefore I was able to comply with my promise. I went straight from Washington to Nevis.

Soon after my arrival at Nevis Prof. R. M. Washburn, of the State university, who was at Nevis to lecture in the interest of farming, seized me by the arm. The professor was aglow with enthusiasm and requested me to follow him. I could understand that some grand object lesson was in store. Sure enough, he led me to a hall and had me stand where I could overlook an exhibit of agricultural and horticultural products, and also various kinds of needlework, drawings and other industrial products of the people there. "This," he said, "is one of many fairs that I have attended. Behold this exhibit."

[omitted]

[Page 1446]

The village folks, joined by their neighbor farmers, had collected together the evidences of the intelligence and thrift of the exhibitors the productivity and adaptability of the climate and soils for certain agricultural and horticultural products. It was, of course, not the first such exhibit that I had seen, but just then, direct from the Nation's Capital and the doings of Congress, the importance of what had been suggested to me and my own observations along the lines of human industry everywhere, linked in their relations directly and indirectly with the acts of Congress, made an extraordinary and vivid impression on my mind.

Is all this to make humanity more prosperous and happy? If it were so, it would be well, for above all things it is important to conserve to men and women the products that result from their intelligence and industry. That is the hope of the world. But that kind of conservation has been almost wholly neglected. Congress appropriates more to protect the hogs, cattle, and dumb animals than it does to preserve satisfactory conditions among the people.

The things that are taking place at Nevis in a way are taking place in the agricultural districts everywhere. It is being supplemented in the factories, in the mines, on the railways, and in the various industries where people are working to produce the necessities of life. To conserve these people and their children in health, prosperity, and happiness is the real conservation problem — to conserve the products of their own energy for their own use, and not for the purpose of giving it to pay interest on credit supported by themselves, but paid to bankers and others. That is the real problem that is before Congress in the consideration of the currency bill, but the currency bill fails in this respect. It simply gives the bankers the privilege of extending credits to charge the people interest on, while the Government is to support it.

I doubt that any Member would intentionally wrong the people, but it is known that the Money Trust is adroit in its plans to defeat those who dare to oppose it. **Members who oppose it are subject to all kinds of attempts to injure their reputation back in their districts.** The trusts control some of the newspapers and have them and other agents at work. These libel, slander, and hatch up all sorts of schemes in the hopes to start the people themselves to making unfavorable comments about Members whom the trusts wish to remove from Congress. But the people have discovered this and are not often fooled by them. So now the Money Trust has supplementary schemes, and try them out with some success in molding legislation. This scheme has been to make the people believe that the trusts are opposed to the very thing that the trusts favor. It is assumed that the people will favor what the trusts openly claim to be against. Smoothly the Money Trust has played a game of fake opposition to allay the suspicions of the public while it put through Congress its plan to shape this new bill. Members have voted for it who never would have done so if they did not believe the people wanted it. **One of the shrewdest things that has, occurred in connection with this bill was a speech made within the walls of this Capitol by a very distinguished person in opposition to the bill. I believe that speech to have been made for the very, purpose of giving it a better chance to pass.**

The new law will create inflation whenever the trusts want inflation. It may not do so immediately, but the trusts want a period of inflation, because all the stocks they hold have gone down because the people got suspicious of them in the investigations and refused to buy. They have been dropping for a long time. Now, if the trusts can get another period of inflation they figure they can unload the stocks on the people at high prices during the excitement and then bring on a panic and buy them back at low prices. Formerly they worked the stocks up and down several times a year to fleece the people, but the people have been keeping out of stocks for a while. Excitement, it is hoped by the trusts, will bring them back.

Several in both House and Senate voted against this bill because their votes were not necessary to carry it. But if it stood in danger of losing, like the 23 Democrats who a few sessions since came to the rescue of the standpat Republicans to save as much of the gag rules as possible, here too, I repeat, if it were necessary to save from defeat this Money Trust bill, there would be a sacred and trusted "23," so to term it, on hand to help pass the bill.

This act establishes the most gigantic trust on earth, such as the Sherman Antitrust Act would dissolve if Congress did not by this act expressly create what by that act it prohibited. When the President signs this act the invisible government by the money power, proven to exist by the Money Trust investigation, will be legalized.

The bill establishes regional banks to be owned by the other banks. The United States Treasury collects taxes from the people. These it will deposit in the regional banks, but will get no interest or at most very little. These banks will be controlled by nine directors — three of them selected by the Federal Reserve Board and six by the banks. That will give the banks full control, with the privilege of the three other directors to look on and see how slick they will do it. It will work out in about this way: All the taxes collected from the people by the United States officers will be deposited in the regional banks. Those of the people who have any money will deposit it in the local banks. The people who are compelled to borrow will go to the local banks and borrow that money. It will be the same money that their neighbors and their beloved Government, the United States, deposited in the banks. They will give their notes for these loans to the local banks. The local banks will send the notes to the regional banks which they own. The regional banks will take them to the people's Government, the United States, and have some more money printed. This the local banks will get. This may be loaned to manufacturers, merchants, etc., and their notes taken, and these notes again may be sent to the regional banks and go through the same process to get some more money from the United States — and so on the endless chain will continue. That is the financial end of it. Then comes the domestic. Of course we all know, and I shall explain the process later, that all this interest is added to the price of the things we buy, or if we are the original producer, subtracted from the things we sell, or in case we are wage workers it is subtracted from our wages or made up by extra hours of work. The consequence is that the farmer's wife, the wage worker's wife, and others wives who are not supported by the usury system, are compelled to work long, long days in their domestic toil, and their daughters are sent to be the servants of the usurers, and their husbands are kept in the field, at the bench, or other place of toll, all to pay the usury that has been supported by the old system and enlarged on by this new fraud. When I hear politicians talk about a progressive administration and then review this bill, which is to be a Christmas gift to the Money Trust, I pity the innocent children all over this land — defenseless they are, but the burden created by this act in lieu of a promise for liberation from the false old system that has made 94,000,000 people industrial slaves, is a shame that should make the administration seek its own oblivion.

The trusts may have temporary prosperity by reason of this act. They control the banking interests. This is a great grant to the banks immensely more than they had a right to expect even from a subservient Congress. But their triumph is the loss of the people. The people may not know it immediately, but the day of reckoning is only a few years removed. The trusts will soon realize that they have gone too far even for their own good. This act places the jackscrew and the vise completely within their hands, and the squeezing process which they will apply to force the last bit of energy from the toilers to enrich the wealthy will go to the point of maddening the people.

Since there is no hope to stop this Congress from passing this bill, I shall discuss a few of the principles involved and the ways and means for the people to make a declaration of independence to relieve themselves from the money power. ***This they will be able to do by taking control of Congress.***

The bill is of such far-reaching injustice that I feel it my duty, preliminary to considering some fundamental principles involved, to make some observations on the system that has made it possible to prevent Members of Congress from preparing a good bill and forcing a vote upon it.

The Money Trust caused the 1907 panic, and thereby forced Congress to create a National Monetary Commission, which drew a bill in the interests of the Money Trust, but Congress did not dare to pass the bill as coming from that Commission. The main features of that bill, however, were copied into this bill. In 1912 I made a speech predicting that that would be done, and, further, that the Money Trust would cause a money stringency in order to force its bill through Congress. All this has now taken place. This bill is passed by Congress as a Christmas present to the Money Trust.

The political cowardice existing in this Capitol will prevent adequate reform until the people themselves realize more fully the burden that is placed on them by the interest, dividends, rents, and profits allowed by law, and collected by banks and others who control centralized wealth.

[Page 1447]

The money power overawes the legislative and executive forces of the Nation and of the States. I have seen these forces exerted during the different stages of this bill. It has convinced me that the people can secure no help from Congress until public sentiment is directed to a specific bill in the people's interests. There has been a strong sentiment for reform, but it has not been directed to a specific remedy, and, therefore, the Money Trust has taken advantage of the sentiment, and under disguise has put forward its own bill — the bill that is about to become a law. Had the people presented a bill and demanded Congress to pass it, Congress would not dare to pass this bill as a Christmas present to the Money Trust.

Even the House bill was a vicious bill, and I so stated it before, but it could hardly be worse than the old law. It might be better, but the Senate amendments have completely legalized a gigantic trust and reenacted the old Aldrich-Vreeland emergency currency act of 1908. It shows how persistent the trusts are to control those in power. The

Democrats here then, and many of them are still in Congress, all voted against that bill, and now when in power all of the Democratic Senators and all but two of the Democratic Representatives in the house vote for it.

The grandiloquent attempt is being made to make the people believe that the control of the money system is being taken out of the banks and placed in the Government. There never was a more deceptive attempt than this. The people are principally interested in how to get money when they need it and what it will cost them. This bill empowers the banks to get more money on the credit of the people so as to collect more interest.

[Omitted]

[Page 1459]

MR. TEMPLE …

The bill in its new form provides for sounder currency than when it passed the House. It then required that the new bank notes should be supported by a reserve requirement of 33 1/3 per cent in gold or lawful money. Now, that reserve must be 40% in gold only. In its old form the bill made no provision for redeeming notes in gold. The present bill makes them redeemable in gold at the Treasury of the United States. It would be better still if the issuing banks, as well as the Treasury were compelled to redeem them in gold instead of gold or lawful money, but the provision for any redemption is gold is a decided improvement. The bill in its new form also by inserting two to three brief clauses defines somewhat more clearly the commercial paper eligible for rediscount, and thereby adds somewhat to the not too secure safeguards against inflation.

[Omitted]

MR UNDERWOOD. …

Therefore I congratulate the wisdom of this committee in recognizing that fact and in the beginning establishing a Government control of this system that would represent the borrowers of money and enable the people of America to secure the medium of exchange at reasonable rates of interest at all times. I think that that is probably the greatest reform that has been worked out in this bill, and yet a reform that will not endanger any banking interest; for were this Federal reserve board that is organized for the purpose of protecting the rights of the American people to be so drastic in its management of this system or so unwise as to abandon the field of safe banking it would but wreck the system and injure the people that it is supposed to represent. Therefore I believe that this board will carefully and safely manage this system, not only in the interest of the American people and low interest rates, but also will have the wisdom to see that the great banking interests of the country are properly safeguarded and protected.

We have heard in recent years of a Money Trust. It is difficult to define what a Money Trust is or where it exists, but we do know that there has been at various times a control of the surplus money of this country in the hands of a few men, and that has largely grown out of the fact that the law upon the statute books forced the reserves of this country, or a great majority of them, to go to one great city in America to be assembled in banks that you could count on the fingers of your two hands, and necessarily that brought about the control of our financial system by a few men. One of the great reforms accomplished in the bill is the taking of the reserves out of the reserve centers and scattering them to at least eight regional reserve banks possibly more, placing them in banks that will be under governmental supervision where the country bank or the local bank would be assured in time of stress and time of peril of being able to vitalize and utilize its reserves that are held for emergency purposes. ***The other great reform, and one that has been needed in this country for a half century, is in the fact that at last we are to have a currency that will respond to the business needs of the country. We are to have an elastic currency that will enable the people of this country, when money is demanded to transact business, to go to the machinery that is provided by this bill, to go to an institution that is authorized by law to give them the currency that the business needs of the country demand and to retire it when it is no longer needed in circulation.***

> ***The difficulty which the great business men in the country have labored under for many years has been that they have had to go hand in hand to the owner of money and ask as a privilege to transact business This bill provides a machinery by which legitimate business needs may have the money with which to transact business as a matter of right and not as a matter of privilege.***
>
> With these reforms written on the statute books, I have a firm conviction that the great banking interests of the country will accept this bill, that it will be a real boon to the people of the United States, that it will relieve any stringency that may exist in monetary circles today, that it will oil the wheels of commerce, that it will promote business enterprise and encourage business development. I believe that the era of dull times and inactivity of business will pass away tomorrow when the President of the United States signs this bill.

[Omitted]

[Page 1460]

Mr. HAYES. Mr. Speaker, I yield to the gentleman from Wyoming [Mr. MONDELL].

MR. MONDELL. Mr. Speaker, I would suggest to my friend from Alabama [Mr. HEFLIN] that a man does not need a glass eye to see the mice and crickets in this measure, the perils and pitfalls it contains. I can not in three minutes catalogue, much less discuss, the many fundamental and fatal features of the bill. One of them is that provision which places upon the American people the enormous burden that ought to be borne by the bankers of final responsibility for the redemption of the notes that are to be issued. Another is the provision of the bill under which the organization, the Federal board, that is to control all the banking credit of the country may be a purely partisan board, and is likely to be such. Another is the provision under which that board, so constituted, has such vast powers that it becomes in effect a great partisan, political, central banking institution. So much for some of the faults of commission. One of the fundamental errors of omission is the fact that there is no adequate provision in the bill for the retirement of notes, and, therefore, there is a serious threat and danger of inflation. Another, that it does not adequately provide for farm loans, in that there is absent from the bill a provision contained in the bill when it passed the House for savings departments in national banks.

These and many more reasons are all sufficient to justify a vote against the bill. But there are other reasons, Mr. Chairman. The question of the currency is a nonpartisan one and it should be so treated, but the majority willed to treat it as a partisan question. They took it into a secret and binding caucus, which, by confessions of men on the other side, was largely controlled by the President and members of his Cabinet. It came to the floor with every Member on that side caucus bound, and not a vote has been or will be taken in this House on this bill which reflects the free and untrammeled action of Members on that side. It follows, therefore, that a vote for this bill is not only a vote in favor of all the faults and defects of the measure, but it is also an indorsement and approval of all of the vicious and unjustifiable partisan methods of consideration which are largely responsible for the faults of the measure.

THE SPEAKER. The time of the gentleman has expired.

[Page 1461]

MR. WILLIS. Mr. Speaker, I have listened with a great deal of interest to the prophecies and rhapsodies coming from the other side of the chamber, but the difficulty about those prophecies is that the prophets do not agree. The gentleman from Pennsylvania [Mr. PALMER] said a little while ago that when this bill passed this House it was a good bill, and then when it passed the Senate it was a better bill, and yet standing right there at the reading desk just few hours ago the gentleman from Virginia [Mr. GLASS], in charge of this bill, said that when it passed the Senate not only was it not a better bill but the enactment of it into law would have been a "calamity" and would have resulted, to quote his enact words, "in a perfect saturnalia of inflation." Mr. Speaker, I believe the chairman was stating the truth with reference to this legislation

Section 16 of this bill contains enough unsound financial provisions to bring industrial and financial calamity upon the country; or, as the chairman of the Committee on Banking and Currency has stated, sufficient to lead "to a perfect saturnalia of inflation," as he so eloquently and aptly described when referring to the provisions of the Senate bill. It is to be observed that the essential provisions of section 16 remain in the conference report substantially as they were in the bill passed by the Senate. This section 16 as it stands in the conference report in part is as follows:

> SEC. 16. Federal reserve notes, to be issued at the discretion of the Federal reserve board for the purpose of making advances to Federal reserve banks through the Federal reserve agents as hereinafter set forth and for no other purpose, are hereby authorized. The said notes shall be obligations of the United States, and shall be receivable by all national and member banks and Federal reserve banks and for all taxes, customs, and other public dues. They shall be redeemed in gold on demand at the Treasury Department of the United States, in the city of Washington, D. C., or in gold or lawful money at any Federal reserve bank.

There are at least four provisions in the portion of the section quoted which are fraught with the gravest consequences to the financial prosperity of the country. First, it is stated that these notes are to be issued "at the discretion of the Federal reserve board." It will be seen by referring to section 10 that this Federal reserve board is a partisan organization. In the bill which passed the House it was provided that not more than one of the four appointive members of the Federal reserve board should be selected from any one Federal reserve district, nod not more than two of them should be of the same political party. It should be noticed that this provision relative to a bipartisan board has been stricken out of the House bill, and in the measure that is now before the House it is provided that the federal reserve board shall consist of five members to be appointed by the President of the United States, by and with the advice and consent of the Senate, with two additional members in the persons of the Secretary of the Treasury and the Comptroller of the Currency. From this provision of the proposed law it is quite evident that all seven members of the Federal reserve board will be members of the same political party.

At any, rate, there is nothing in the law to prevent it, and it is not overstating the case to say that as this law must be interpreted in view of the action of the Senate in striking out the provision in the House bill which provided that not more than two of the appointive members should be of the same political party, it is clear that the purpose of the legislation now proposed to be enacted is to make this Federal reserve board a partisan organization.

Now, then, considering section 10 in connection with section 16, let us see what results we obtain. Here we have a board of seven men, all appointed by the President and undoubtedly all of the same political party. Now, what power have they under the terms of section 16? Quoting again from this section, it is found that Federal reserve notes are to be issued "at the discretion of the Federal reserve board." So far as this proposed legislation is concerned, there is absolutely no limitation upon the amount of notes which may be issued. Herein resides the possibility of inflation. Of course it is admitted that provision is made for a reserve fund of 40 per cent, together with the commercial paper put up as collateral, but I submit this, Mr. Speaker, that it is unwise, unsound, and will prove to be disastrous legislation to give to any board such immense power over the control of the circulating medium of this country as is contemplated in the portion of section 16 which I have just quoted. There ought to be in this bill somewhere a positive limitation upon the amount of circulating medium which can be issued. To omit such a salutary provision is to invite the financial disaster which has always followed in the wake of an inflated paper circulation. It certainly is a most interesting coincidence that now, as always in the past, in the face of threatening financial disaster — when news is coming in from every quarter of the closing down of mills, of the organization of the armies of the unemployed, of the actions of various municipalities in taking emergency steps to furnish employment to workingmen now out of employment but who heretofore have been busily employed in the mills and factories and mines — at such a time, in the face of an undoubted industrial lethargy, it seems most peculiar that the party in control of the Government should resort to the same measure to which it has always resorted under such occasions, namely, that of inflation of the currency. What we want in this country at the present moment is not more paper money, but more busy mills. Not more importation of foreign products, but better production at home at better wages, with better protection for our own farmers, our own laborers, and our own markets. Not inflated credit, but more men at work here in America at good wages to furnish a market for the farmers' products. The resort to such financial nostrums as are illustrated by this bill will be only a temporary stimulant and in the end will work much harm to the producers of the country. This then, is my first serious objection to this bill — that it puts into the hands of seven men appointed for political purposes the power to say what the amount of the circulating medium of this country shall be. The financial life of our people is too great a stale to rest upon the attire edict of any such body of men, however able and distinguished they may be.

In the second place it is provided in this section 16 that "said notes shall be obligations of the United States." I object to this provision, Mr. Speaker, because these is no good reason why these notes which are to be issued to the Federal reserve banks and are to be circulated by them for their profit should not be the obligations of the banks instead of the obligation of the United States. ***These few lines of section 16 disclose the whole purpose of this legislation. Shorn of its verbiage it amounts simply to this : That the credit of the United States is to be loaned to a certain special class for the benefit of that class.*** Is there any good reason why the credit of the great Government of the United States should be loaned to these Federal reserve banks which would not apply equally well to other classes and business organizations of this country? ***If the Government of the United States is to go into the business of loaning its credit to various persons, corporations, and associations, why should it not loan it to the farmers and workingmen of the country as well as to certain special favorites known as Federal reserve banks?***

In my judgment the provision which undertakes to saddle the obligation of redeeming these notes upon the Government of the United States, thus making them in fact direct obligations of the Federal Government, is entirely unjustifiable. I believe that if the American people understood that the effect of this legislation was to saddle upon their shoulders the obligation of redeeming the notes issued by this federal reserve board to Federal reserve banks they would rise up almost to a man and oppose this legislation. Since these notes are to be issued to the federal reserve banks for the profit of those organizations they ought to be the obligations of those banks. It ought to be the duty of the banks to redeem the notes. No such obligation and no such duty should rest upon the shoulders of the Government: of the United States.

It is provided in the third place, in section 16, that those notes so issued "shall be receivable for all taxes, customs, and other public dues." By this it means that the Federal Government while assuming greater obligations and greater burdens, is deprived of the only source of gold revenue which it has. In other words, while the financial burden of the Federal Government is increased, its ability to carry that burden and discharge that that obligation is decreased. It surely can not be maintained that this is sound financial legislation.

In the Fourth place, it is provided that while these notes of the Federal reserve bank shall be redeemable "in gold on demand at the Treasury Department of the United States in the city of Washington, D. C.," that they may be redeemed "in gold or lawful money" at any Federal reserve bank. Why this distinction? If the notes are to be made redeemable in gold at the bands of the Government of the United States why should not the Federal reserve banks, for whose benefit and profit the notes are to be issued, at the same time be required to redeem their obligations in gold? But they are given the special privilege of redeeming their notes in "gold or in lawful money." It seems to me, Mr. Speaker, that these four objections lodged against section 16 are insuperable. If we enact such legislation as is provided in this section we are flying in the face of all the facts of the financial history of this country and of the rest of the civilized world.

[Page 1464]

The question was taken; and there were — yeas 298, nays 60, and not voting 76, as follows:

Yeas — 298.

[Omitted]

Nays — 60

Anderson	Austin	Bartholdt
Browne, WI	Browning	Butler
Cailaway	Danforth	Dye
Frenc	Gardne	Good
Green, IA	Greene	Greene, VT
Greis	Guernse	Hamilton, MI
Hamilton, NY	Hawle	Haye
Hinds	Howell	Humphrey
Johnson, UT	Johnson, WA	Kahn
Keiste	Kennedy, RI	Langham
Langley	Lewis, PA	Lindberg
McGuire, OK	McLaughlin	Mann
Mondell	Moore	Morgan, OK
Morin	Parke	Patton, PA
Payne	Platt	Prouty
Roberts	Roger	Scott
Slemp	Smith, ID	Steenerson
Switzer	Towner	Vare
Volstead	Wallin	Willis
Winslow	Witherspoon	Woods

Footnotes

[1] Furness, William Henry III, *The Island of Stone Money* (J. B. Lippincott Company: Phildadephia, 1910), p 93, 96–98.

[2] *Ibid.* p 98-100

[3] Quigley, Carroll, *Tragedy and Hope* (Macmillan: New York, 1966), p 325.

[4] On page 3 of his book *Honest Money* (Dominion Press: Ft Worth, 1986), Gary North recalls a time in 1985 when there was a sharp increase in the "cash" in circulation. At Gary North's suggestion, one of Congressman Dr. Ron Paul's research assistants contacted the Federal Reserve to find out if they thought this was due to Mexicans hoarding dollars – or, more properly, Federal Reserve Notes. The congressional staff member was told by two of the Federal Reserve's staff economists, one of whom was a specialist in the Mexican economy, that it was quite unlikely that Mexicans were hoarding dollars, when they could simply take their cash dollars to the bank, exchange them for pesos, deposit the pesos, and receive interest on the deposit. At the time of this conversation the peso was trading at 250 pesos to the dollar. Within one week the peso had fallen to 500 pesos to the dollar. Anyone following the advice of that expert would have lost half his money in less than a week. It seems as if the illiterate Mexican peasants were smarter than the "pedigreed" economists.

[5] William Gouge in his excellent book on money notes: "Some fancy that it is the authority of Government that gives money its value. But the true value of money, as measured by the amount of goods for which it will honestly exchange, cannot be affected by edicts of Princes or acts of Parliament. Monarchs and Ministers may alter the weight of coins, or lessen their purity; but they cannot make a coin containing an half of an ounce of pure silver, worth as much as a coin containing an ounce. The stamp of the state is a mere certificate of the weight and fineness of the piece." [Gouge, William *A Short History of Paper Money and Banking in the United States* (T. W. Ustick,: Philadelphia, PA, 1833 Reprinted 1968 by Augustus M. Kelley) p. 9]

[6] Hepburn, A. Barton, *Contest for Sound Money*, (Greenwood Press: New York, 1968. Originally published, 1903) p 7-8.

[7] North, Gary, *Honest Money*, (Dominion Press: Ft. Worth, Texas and Thomas Nelson: Nashville, TN) p 9, 10.

[8] Ibid. p. 10

[9] Ibid, p 11.

[10] Gouge, William *A Short History of Paper Money and Banking in the United States* (T. W. Ustick,: Philadelphia, PA, 1833 Reprinted 1968 by Augustus M. Kelley) p. 10.

[11] Hazlitt, Henry, *Economics in One Easy Lesson*, (Arlington House Publishers: Westport, CT, 1978) p 1.

[12] John Kenneth Galbraith said in *The Age of Uncertainty* (Houghton Mifflin: Boston, 1977), Chapter 6, *The Rise and Fall of Money*, p 166, "Then came the second Amsterdam discovery, although the principle was known elsewhere. The deposits so created did not need to be left idly in the bank. They could be lent. The borrower then had a deposit he could spend. ... Money, spendable money, had been created. Let no one rub his or her eyes. It's still being done—every day. The creation of money by a bank is as simple as this, so simple, I've often said, that the mind is slightly repelled."

[13] Ah, but I would invest it, you are thinking. However, even if you invest the money, it is still being put into circulation. From the perspective of the economy, it does not matter if you spend it on a cruise, or buy a business — both increase the money in circulation.

[14] These merchants may not have borne the full brunt of the devalued red rocks if they immediately traded them. But in that case, it only serves to distribute the loss among many merchants. Individually or collectively, someone must pay for the "bargain" experienced by our friend who was able to obtain both the suit and the computer.

[15] This section and the next section on Unequal Distribution Effects are somewhat technical and may be skipped without loss of continuity.

[16] Some might think that this is not a problem because the courier has money, which he did not previously have, that will be spent into the economy. The answer is that this is entirely offset by the fact that retailer

has less money to spend into the economy. In addition, the time the courier spent transporting the money, was time that was not available for true productive activity; such as developing a better mousetrap. For a fuller explanation, see Henry Hazlitt, *Economics in One Lesson* (Arlington House Publishers: Westport, 1979), p23ff.

[17] Note that this receipt contains a contract. Beginning at the very top of the note in fine print it reads: "This certifies that there has been deposited in the Treasury of the [begin big print over picture]United States of America [[big print under picture] ten dollars on gold coin [begin fine print at bottom of note] payable to the bearer on demand." As we will see later, this gold certificate is an honest paper receipt, contrary to later notes.

[18] The reason is that the people defrauded by duplicate receipts do not realize they are being defrauded; nor is there a direct link between the criminal and the victim as there is in the hypothetical rental car scenario. Instead, the blame for economic ills is placed on the government, in general, and the president in particular.

[19] Quoted in *The Creature from Jekyll Island*, by G. Edward Griffin (American Opinion: Appleton, 1994), p 156.

[20] Keynes, John Maynard, *Economic Consequences of the Peace* (Penguin USA, 1988), p 235.

[21] John Galbraith sets the ratio at 1000 billion to one in his book *The Age of Uncertainty*, (Boston, MA: Houghton Mifflin, 1977), p 190.

[22] McManus, John F., *Financial Terrorism* (Appleton, WI: The John Birch Society, 1993), p. 125.

[23] *Wall Street Journal*, June 6, 1995. p 1.

[24] Dewey, Davis Rich, Ph.D., *Financial History of the United States* (New York: Longmans, Green & Co., 1922), p 21.

[25] Labaree, Leonard W., ed., *The Papers of Benjamin Franklin* (Yale University Press: New Haven, 1960) Vol. 2, p 159. Quoted in *The Creature from Jekyll Island*, by G. Edward Griffin (American Opinion: Appleton, 1994) p 158.

[26] Gouge , William M., *A Short History of Paper Money and Banking in the United States* (T.W. Ustick: Philadelphia, 1833, Reprinted Augustus M. Kelley Publishers, 1968), Part II, p 27.

[27] Hepburn, A. Barton, *Contest for Sound Money*, (Greenwood Press: New York, 1968. Originally published, 1903) p 55-57.

[28] Journal Continental Congress as quoted in Hepburn, p 56.

[29] Thomas Jefferson, Observations on the article Etatis-Unis Prepared for the Encyclopedia, June 22, 1786, from Writings (G.P. Putnam's Sons: New York, 1894), Vol. IV, p. 165.

[30] Atwood, Harry, *The Constitution Explained,* (Destiny Publishers: Merrimac, Massachusetts, 1927), p 3.

[31] *Ibid.*, p. 4.

[32] Gouge, Part II, p. 28.

[33] Bancroft, George, *A Plea for the Constitution* (Harper: New York , 1886), as quoted in Griffin, *The Creature From Jekyl Island,* p 30, 43-44, 82.

[34] *Ibid.*, p 158.

[35] Saussy, Frederick Tupper, *The Miracle on Main Street* (Spencer Judd Publishers: Sewanee, Tennessee, 1980), p 32.

[36] Mint Act of April 2, 1792, Section 20 [Congressional Record, Second Congress, Session 1, Chapter 16, 1792], p 250.

[37] North, Gary, *Honest Money* (Dominion Press: Fort Worth, 1986), p 52.

[38] Mint Act of April 2, 1792, Section 19 [Congressional Record, Second Congress, Session 1, Chapter 16, 1792], p 250.

[39] Saussy, p 36.

[40] "Just What is Money? Does Anyone Know," Louis Rukeyser, *St Louis Globe Democrat*, June 1, 1982, Section C, page 1.

[41] The article continues, "And until they do, the much publicized attempts to get the US money supply under control are as unlikely to be successful as a brain surgery performed by a kindergartner." Ibid.

[42] "Washington Wire", *Wall Street Journal*, September 24, 1971, p1.

[43] Abraham, Larry, *Call It Conspiracy* (Double A Publications: Seattle, 1985), p 273.

[44] Quigley, Carroll, *Tragedy and Hope* (MacMillan: New York, 1966), p 950.

[45] *New York Times*, Sunday, May 3, 1931, Section C, p 1. This estimate taken from the article covering the death of George F. Baker, a stockholder in the Federal Reserve Bank.

[46] Griffin, G. Edward, *The Creature From Jekyll Island (American Opinion: Appleton, 1994)*, p 4.

[47] Chernow, Ron, *The House of Morgan* (Atlantic Monthly Press: New York, 1990), p 90. Chernow notes that Standard Oil pumped so much money into the National City Bank that by 1893 it was the largest bank in New York. He also notes that two of James Stillman's daughters married two of William Rockefeller's sons. William Rockefeller was the younger brother of John D. and a founding partner of Standard Oil and James Stillman was the president of National City Bank.

[48] "From Farm Boy to Financier," by Frank Vanderlip, *The Saturday Evening Post,* Feb 9, 1933, pp 25, 70.

[49] And this is the condemnation, that light is come into the world, and men loved darkness rather than light, because their deeds were evil. For every one that doeth evil hateth the light, neither cometh to the light, lest his deeds should be reproved. But he that doeth truth cometh to the light, that his deeds may be made manifest, that they are wrought in God John 3:19-21

[50] Congressional Record, House of Representatives, 63rd Congress, December 22, 1913, p 1430. See Appendix 2.

[51] Griffin, p 12.

[52] Krooss, Herman E., Ed. *Documentary History of Banking and Currency in the United States.* (Chelsea House: New York, 1969), Vol III, p 2101, 2102. Address of Nelson W. Aldrich, Chairman of the National Monetary Commission, Before the Annual Convention of the American Bankers' Association, at New Orleans, Tuesday, November 21, 1911.

[53] Congressional Record, House of Representatives, 63rd Congress, December 22, 1913, p 1446. See Appendix 2.

[54] *New York Times*, Front page headline, December 22, 1913.

[55] This same tactic was used again to pass the General Agreement on Trade and Tariffs (GATT) during the Christmas season in 1994.

[56] Aldrich, in *The Independent*, July 1914.

[57] Congressional Record, House of Representatives, 63rd Congress, December 22, 1913, p 1433. See Appendix 2, The Federal Reserve Act, Sec 7.

[58] Mint Act of April 2, 1792, Section 20, (Congressional Record, 2nd Congress, Session 1, Chapter 16, 1792) p 250.

[59] Murdoch, Lawrence C., *The Hats the Federal Reserve Wears*, (Federal Reserve Bank of Philadelphia, April 1986) p 13. Murdoch is the vice-president and secretary of the Philadelphia branch of the Federal Reserve Bank.

[60] See Federal Reserve Act, Sec. 4, Paragraph 4 and following. A copy of the Act and relevant portions of the congressional record are in Appendix 2.

[61] *Coins and Currency*, Published by the Public Information Department, Federal Reserve Bank of New York (33 Liberty Street, New York, New York 10045), April 1985. p 18.

[62] Of course, the last person could always try to find another person to ignorantly accept the worthless check in exchange for the fruit of his labor. This postpones the inevitable for as long as there are people who are willing to accept the bad check.

[63] Murdoch, Lawrence C., *The Hats the Federal Reserve Wears.* p 6.

[64] Anthony Sutton, *Wall Street and FDR* (New Rochelle, New York: Arlington House, 1975) p 94

[65] Gonczy, Anne Marie L., *Modern Money Mechanics: A Workbook on Bank Reserves and Deposit Expansion*, (Federal Reserve Bank of Chicago, Revised June 19,1992) p 3.

[66] Ibid. p 6.

[67] Ibid. p 7

[68] Modern Money Mechanics, p 6: "It was a small step from printing notes to making book entries crediting deposits of borrowers, which the borrowers could 'spend' by writing checks, thereby printing their own money."

[69] Many books on the Federal Reserve are quick to point out that this ability to generate money is only true of the banking system as a whole and not true of any one bank. Some even call it a paradox. But it is really no paradox at all. If there was only one bank, it would be true of that one bank. To the extent that lower level creditors bank with the first bank, the first bank can indeed loan more than the initial deposit - even in our multi-bank economy. E.g. *The Federal Reserve System: Purposes and Functions*, Board of Governors of the Federal Reserve System, Washington, D. C., 1963, p 74.

[70] Congressional Record, 77th Congress, House of Representatives, Committee on Banking and Currency, Price Control Bill, Wednesday, October 1, 1941, p 1353.

[71] The September 23, 1914 issue of the New York Times gave a list of stockholders of the member banks of the Federal Reserve. Included were such men as James Stillman, Chairman of the Board, National City Bank (The bank of which Vanderlip was President); W. Rockefeller, J. D. Rockefeller, J. S. Rockefeller, A. C. Taylor, J. P. Morgan, H. B. Davison, J. H. Schiff, W. W. Astor, P. N. Warburg, G. F. Baker, A. Barton Hepburn, (author of *Contest For Sound Money*), trustees of Princeton University, Mary Harriman, and others. Recently the Chairman of the Federal Reserve has been getting much more attention in the press. Most people now know who he is.

[72] Murdoch, Lawrence C. *The Hats the Federal Reserve Wears*, (Federal Reserve Bank of Philadelphia, 1986) p 7.

[73] Congressional Record, 77th Congress, House of Representatives, Committee on Banking and Currency, Price Control Bill, Wednesday, October 1, 1941, p 1355. The bill, referred to as H. R. 116, 77th Congress, 1st Session, would have transferred the stock of the Federal Reserve Corporation to the US government.

[74] Ibid., September 30, 1941, p 1338.

[75] Ibid. p 1342.

[76] Even if you don't, Scripture requires that I provide you with 2 or 3 witnesses.

[77] Gonczy, Anne Marie L. and Timothy P. Schilling, *Two Faces of Debt*, (Federal Reserve Bank of Chicago, Fifth Revision, 1992), p 4.

[78] *Two Faces of Debt*, p 2.

[79] Ibid. p 5.

[80] There is a sense in which certain debts could be regarded as assets. If I hold a mortgage, then that would be an asset, compared to owing the mortgage. But there is still a major difference between holding this type of asset and holding the actual asset. The former is only the promise to pay an asset at a future date. The latter is the actual asset. There is a major difference. Ask any creditor who has had a debtor default. Or try to sell your debt asset. See if any investor is willing to buy it at par. You will find that investors will only buy it at a discount. Promissory notes are not the same as assets, unless you are talking to the IRS.

[81] Ibid. p 25.

[82] Immigration of impoverished people has become such a financial burden because the US has become a socialist nation that rewards the unproductive and taxes the productive. We steal by oppressive taxation the wealth of the productive and give it to the impoverished who do not have the skills to be productive with it. At the same time, we do not allow people who are not worth the minimum wage to work for what they are worth. Consequently, it becomes very difficult (or very expensive) for unskilled people to acquire necessary skills. If we allowed them to work for what they are worth and did not pay them for not working, the diligent would be both empowered and motivated to become productive citizens, strengthening the economy instead of dragging it down. This opportunity is what drew so many immigrants to America in the late 19th and early 20th centuries.

[83] Including the widower and anyone else on a fixed income.

[84] Josepus, Flavius, "*Writings of Flavius Josephus,* Tr. by William Whitson, (Kregel Publications, 1960), p 578.

[85]See also Pr 13:23 *Abundant food is in the fallow ground of the poor, but it is swept away by injustice.* Pr 8:36 *He that sins against me wrongs his own soul; all they that hate me love death.* Lev 18:24-28, Is 24.

[86] For example, all officers in the state of Delaware had to take the following oath: "I, _____ do profess faith in God the Father, and in Jesus Christ His only Son, and in the Holy Ghost, one God, blessed for evermore; and 1 do acknowledge the holy scriptures of the Old and New Testament to be given by divine inspiration." In Pennsylvania all officers, including sheriffs, all legislators, and everyone serving in the courts were required to profess faith in Jesus Christ and confess and acknowledge the "One Almighty and eternal God, to be the Creator, Upholder, and Ruler of the world;" Frame of Government, 1682. Quoted in *Sources of Our Liberties,* Edited by Richard Perry, [Chicago, American Bar Foundation, 1978].

[87] Many pastors have accommodated themselves to this restriction by teaching that the Scriptures have nothing to say about "political" issues such as the qualifications for civil office or the way to fight a war.

[88] The church is to be teaching people to "observe all things that I have commanded you." (Mtt 28:20) Since Scripture has much to say regarding the civil magistrate, the church ought to have much to say about who might be qualified and who is not qualified for civil office.

[89] Proverbs 22:6.

[90] This is not to deny that children are individuals and have different personalities, interests, and gifts which must be nurtured.

[91] Psalm 78, Proverbs 22:6, I Timothy 3:4.

[92] Genesis 18:19 For I know him, that he will command his children and his household after him, and they shall keep the way of the LORD, to do justice and judgment; *that the LORD may bring upon Abraham that which he hath spoken of him.*

[93] McIhany, William, II *The Tax Exempt Foundations* (Westport, CT: ArlingtonHouse, 1980), p 60 -61.

[94] Interestingly enough Quigley touches on this saying, "...the disintegration of the middle class arose from a failure to transfer its outlook to its children. This failure was thus a failure of education....

Since our education system has been organized as a mechanism for indoctrination of the young in middle-class ideology.... ...[I]t has been more concerned with instilling attitudes and behavior than with intellectual training." Quigley, p 1249.

[95] Chisholm, Brock; *American Journal of Psychiatry*; 1948; 104; p. 543-547.

[96] But thou, O LORD, shalt laugh at them; thou shalt have all the heathen in derision. Ps 59:8.

[97] The declaration: "You are my Son, today I have begotten You," refers to the time of Christ's full manifestation as the eternal Son of God at his resurrection. It does not mean that the second person of the Godhead has a beginning.

The Psalmist is here declaring that He who has been hidden in the bosom of the Father from all eternity and who was revealed in types and shadows under the old administration of the Covenant will now be made manifest to the whole world. His glory will be revealed. This manifestation began with his incarnation. The Apostle John says, "And the Word was made flesh, and dwelt among us, (and we beheld his glory, the glory as of the only begotten of the Father,) full of grace and truth. John 1:14

This manifestation climaxed in Christ's resurrection from the dead. Paul says that our Lord Jesus Christ was declared to be Son of God with power by the resurrection from the dead. "And we declare unto you glad tidings, how that the promise which was made unto the fathers, God has fulfilled the same unto us their children, in that he has raised up Jesus again; as it is also written in the second psalm, 'You are my Son, today I have begotten you.' " Acts 13:32,33.

[98] "And now, Lord, behold their threatenings: and grant unto your servants, that with all boldness they may speak your word." Acts 4:29.

[99] There is little difference between Harry Emerson Fosdick saying that Jonah is a parable that teaches truth — but no one was actually swallowed by a fish, and Meredith Kline saying that Genesis 1 is a framework to teach us truth — but the days were not actually days.

[100] Psalm 127:3b,4 (KJV).

[101] Westminster Larger Catechism, Q105; *What are the sins forbidden in the first commandment?*; "… the not having and avouching him for God, and our God; …"

[102] Westminster Larger Catechism, Q109; *What are the sins forbidden in the second commandment?*; "… tolerating a false religion; …"

[103] For the unbelieving husband is sanctified by the wife, and the unbelieving wife is sanctified by the husband: else were your children unclean; but now are they holy. (1 Corinthians 7:14).

[104] *Modern Money Mechanics*, Chicago Federal Reserve, 1992, p11.